Path To Wisdom

Path To Wisdom

Introducing Western Philosophy

Dr. James Mittelstadt

PARTRIDGE

A Penguin Random House Company

ISBN: Hardcover   978-1-4828-9132-4
       Softcover   978-1-4828-9131-7
       Ebook   978-1-4828-9133-1

To order additional copies of this book, contact
Toll Free 800 101 2657 (Singapore)
Toll Free 1 800 81 7340 (Malaysia)
orders.singapore@partridgepublishing.com

www.partridgepublishing.com/singapore

CONTENTS

INTRODUCTION

The focus of this book is on early Western philosophy. It is obvious that there are other ancient and important strains of philosophy that are also highly significant in the development of universal philosophical thought. For example, I mention the ancient philosophies of India and China. These philosophical beginnings influenced the cultures of East Asia and the Far East throughout many centuries, and their basic ideas still influence many cultures in that area of the world. This book concentrates on the philosophical origins that have influenced Western culture for centuries.

Primarily, the origins began in ancient Greece, spread to many countries by Hellenism after Alexander the Great, expanded, and added to even more by way of Rome and its empire.

I explain the essential kernels of this path to wisdom in simple and understandable language.

I am grateful to Father Clement Wartman PhD, who was a Redemptorist priest and professor of philosophy. He taught for many decades, interrupted only by his service during World War II. He served as a military chaplain in the armed services during those years.

I am indebted to him for opening my intellectual eyes to the wonders of philosophy, especially in the area of Aristotelian Thomistic philosophy.

CHAPTER ONE

Philosophy/Wisdom

The word *philosophy* comes from a Greek word that simply means "love of wisdom." In a universal sense, in the past, it meant a pressing and constant desire to understand what wisdom is and then to become a wise person through this knowledge. In Eastern cultures, to grasp the true meaning of wisdom was to become "enlightened." For centuries, both in the East and in the West, it had been taken for granted that becoming a true philosopher demanded a certain quality of disciplined, contemplative thought and a special way of living out one's life.

A Jewish sage, writing thousands of years ago, described this search in these poetic words:

> Wisdom is brilliant, she never fades.
>> By those who love her, she is readily seen,
>> By those who seek her, she is readily found.
>> She anticipates who desire her by making herself known first.
>> Whoever gets up early to seek her will have no trouble but will find her sitting at the door.
>> Meditating on her is understanding on her is understanding in its perfect form, and anyone keeping awake for her will soon be free from care.
>> For she herself searches everywhere for those who are worthy of her, benevolently appearing to them on their ways, anticipating their every thought.
>> For Wisdom begins with the sincere desire for instruction, anxiety for instruction means loving her, loving

her means keeping her laws, attention to her laws guarantees incorruptibility, and incorruptibility brings us near to God; the desire for Wisdom thus leads to sovereignty.

If then thrones and sceptres delight you, monarchs to the nations, honor Wisdom, so that you may reign forever. (Book of Wisdom)

Nevertheless, it would be misleading to attempt to give a definition of what thinkers today believe philosophy is. There is no longer any common meaning to the word *wisdom*, taken in a universal sense. Are all philosophers wise men? It would seem not. Conversely, are all wise men philosophers? Probably. Still, in a general sense, philosophy can be described as a search for a special kind of insight and wisdom that is broader than the limited wisdom that the specialized fields within the sciences offer. I am talking of the scientific field as such, not of the "scientist." A person of science is also a philosopher—as a person. This seems inescapable.

Philosophy examines the "universal structure of human experience" that is present in any age. It is concerned with the pressing issues *behind* the pressing issues. That is, philosophy is an attempt to discover and understand the first and most basic principles governing universal reality—be these modes of reality, man, the universe, or even God/ gods. Every culture, every age, has its philosophers and philosophies that attempt to formulate these principles.

The psychological and cultural reasons that draw one to commence a life of searching for this special kind of generic wisdom are many. The crises of each age are sometimes the cause, and sometimes the effect, of philosophies. For some individuals, it is simply wonder, curiosity, or a kind of love. A philosopher who lived several hundred years ago says,

> The love towards a thing eternal and infinite alone feeds the mind with a pleasure secure from all pain . . . The greatest good is the knowledge of the union which the mind has with the whole of nature . . . The more the mind knows the more it understands its forces and the order of nature; the more it understands its forces or strength, the better it will be able

to direct itself and lay down the rules for itself . . . this is the whole method. (Baruch Spinoza)

Philosophy/Purpose

For other individuals, philosophy may be a desire to discover some deep, ultimate, and satisfying meaning to answer the question "why" we human beings exist for a time in an ever-changing universe and then disappear. Suffering, pain, sorrow, mental confusion, and the seeming futility of existence can lead one to philosophize. What one philosopher stated over three thousand years ago in the Middle East is similar to the thoughts of some contemporary philosophers:

> Sheer futility . . . sheer futility: everything is futile! What profit can we show for all our toil, toiling under the sun? A generation goes, a generation comes, yet the earth stands firm forever. The sun rises, the sun sets; then to its place it speeds and there it rises . . . All things are wearisome.
> What was, will be again,
> What has been done, will be done again,
> and there is nothing new under the sun!
> Human is no better off than animal—since all is vanity.
> Everything goes to the same place,
> everything comes from the dust,
> everything returns to the dust. (Ecclesiastes)

Ludwig Wittgenstein, a philosopher, expressed the purpose of philosophy in this way: "What is the purpose of philosophy? To show the fly the way out of the glass bottle."

The philosopher, by using human reason and human powers of observation and thought, seeks to enter, if possible, deeper levels of thought. He or she thinks this will lead to a clearer understanding of the ultimate bases and foundations for what might appear to be obvious realities. The philosopher seeks to acquire a special kind of knowledge that will open secret accesses, leading to a deeper and clearer understanding of what it means to be wise and to live wisely.

Such a search for wisdom needs a certain amount of mental freedom to think, study, and contemplate. If one is caught up entirely in the anxious and hurried flow of day-by-day living with its physical and mental burdens, there can be no time for philosophy. As an old proverb states, "He who has no time has no eternity."

An ancient Greek philosopher, Aristotle, describes the task of the philosopher in this way:

> Since we are seeking this knowledge, we must inquire of what kind are the causes and the principles, the knowledge of which is Wisdom. If one were to take the notions we have about the wise man, this might perhaps make the answer more evident. We suppose first, the, that the wise man knows all things, as far as possible, although he has not knowledge of each of them in detail; secondly, that he who can learn things that are difficult, and not easy for man to know, is wise (sense-perception is common to all, and therefore easy and no mark of Wisdom).
>
> The most universal things are on the whole the whole the hardest for men to know; or they are farthest from the senses.
>
> For it is owing to their wonder that men both begin and at first began to philosophize; they wondered originally at the obvious difficulties about the greater matter, e.g. about the phenomena of the moon and those of the sun and of the stars, and about the genesis of the universe. And a man who is puzzled and wonders thinks himself ignorant (whence even the lover of myths is in a sense a lover of Wisdom, for the myth is composed of wonders); therefore since they philosophized in order to escape from ignorance, evidently they were pursuing science in order to know, and not for any utilitarian end.

Philosophy/Truth

In past times, philosophy incorporated into its realm many areas of knowledge and science. For example, natural science was called natural philosophy, astronomy was a part of cosmology, psychology was the philosophy of the mind and soul, and so on. All of these present-day specialized fields were considered branches of philosophy.

Often, a certain amount of preconceptions must be put aside before beginning the study of philosophy. One of them is that philosophy is extremely abstruse and almost occult, a kind of knowledge that reveals its truths only to a few "initiates." Another might think that philosophy is a kind of wisdom that is very abstract and not at all in touch with day-to-day reality; it is some kind of word game that a few people like to play. It is not at all concrete, solid, or down to earth. It leads only to an exasperating mental sterility that is built on "castles in the sky." The problems that it brings up and tries to solve seem to have been repeatedly brought up for thousands of years. The solutions offered by philosophy are often contradictory, monotonous, and devoid of any life.

However, all men and women are bound to philosophize. It is not a game that can be avoided. Decisions about the meaning of one's life, the value of one's daily decisions, or what ought to be done are made daily—sometimes seemingly automatically, sometimes with a great deal of reflection. The very ideas that we hold on to so firmly in today's society concerning the rights of man—for example, the right to equal opportunity for men and women, adequate food and housing, freedom of speech and of religious belief—are all based on some sort of philosophy.

Not all men are philosophers. There is a difference. Perhaps it is a difference in the amount of one's life and psychic energy one gives to philosophy. The philosopher goes to great lengths in coming to grips with the apparent inconsistencies within our human condition. He or she seeks to fulfill the need to establish some order where there is confusion, to bring about some integration where there is fanaticism or disharmony, and to discover some kind of organic whole where everything appears fragmented. Has philosophy ever done that? Can it really do that? On an individual level, the answer is *yes, definitely.* Has this been accomplished on a universal and social level? It would seem that this has been accomplished and is being done sporadically and for a time. Today's trend toward democracy is an example of philosophy in action. Will the trend run itself out at some time in the future? Probably.

The "professional" philosopher is one who has studied the learned works of many (by no means all!) recognized philosophers in a formal academic atmosphere—usually a university. One has academic requirements entitling him or her to be recognized as a professional philosopher. One might then go into an academic field and put this learning to use. That is the usual way today, and it demands an enormous amount of life energy commitment.

There are and have been great philosophers in history who did not acquire academic training in philosophy as such and many who did not even teach philosophy within an academic atmosphere. That is, these men and women started first to "philosophize," wrote down their insights, and then later became and were recognized as outstanding philosophers. They too offered up a great deal of their lives to the "life" of philosophy.

With the advent of modern science and the use of the scientific method, conceptions about the meaning and purpose of philosophy began to vary. Many philosophers began to apply exclusively the research and inquiry methods of the natural sciences to the study of philosophy. Some philosophers wanted to obtain a similar fecundity in the field of philosophy that they saw in the areas of natural sciences, especially mathematics and physics. The purpose of philosophy then began to change for many philosophers. Emphasis shifted for many philosophers (but by no means for all!) from attempting to know and demonstrate what is eternally true.

> The knowledge of necessary and eternal truths is what distinguishes us from mere animals and puts us in possession of reason. (Gottfried Wilhelm Leibniz)

Discovering that which is only probably true and then that which is only relatively true at best are only an examination into what it means to know. **The search for absolute Truth or value gave way to the search for that which is contingently true.** As one **modern** philosopher writes,

> We may rule out ultimate truth as a criterion of philosophical achievement.
>
> The trouble with this definition of philosophy (i.e. a set of propositions that attempts to provide answers . . . about the

ultimate value and meaning of life) is that, even if there is an ultimate truth, nobody is likely to find it or, having found it, to be able to formulate it in neat and tidy propositions. (W. T. Jones)

Philosophy/Knowledge

For all this, philosophy seeks knowledge in a world of ideas. On the one hand, there are philosophers who claim that philosophy seeks an ultimately stable world that differs radically from the constant flow of change that is observed in a transient and temporal world. At the other extreme, there are philosophers who judge that philosophy can only be an ever-changing outlook about an ever-changing world. They claim no other kind of knowledge is provable. Many other philosophers are somewhere between these two extremes.

These differing understandings of what philosophy means depend to a great extent on some psychological functions of man and how they relate to knowledge. Basically these are four:

1) Sensation: perceptions from the senses
2) Intellect: thinking, reasoning, understanding
3) Emotion: feeling
4) Intuition: intellectual insights, immediate grasp of what is true without going through a logical process

Many philosophers tend to assimilate their "first principles" from a mixture of the above. Others choose one or the other of the above functions as the only valid realm of philosophy. Some philosophical theorists intentionally dismiss completely these functions. For them, one particular function is monopolized as the only "philosophizing" function. This is a type of "reductionism."

On the individual level, a certain amount of reductionism, eclecticism, and originality is necessary if one is really to philosophize. After a great amount of reading, understanding, insight, and thought, a philosopher will eventually form his or her own opinions and theories. These opinions will depend on the priority of the "value" that the philosopher places on certain "big" questions that he or she is concerned with.

What are the most important questions to him or to her? Do they deal with God, man, death, pain, suffering, the universe, value systems, permanence, change, freedom, rights, theories of knowledge, environmental issues, or ethics in politics? There is, by the way, a difficulty in one philosopher's trying to convince all other philosophers—or the world—that his or her particular priorities are "self-evidently" the correct priorities.

Philosophy can be described as a way of thinking and a way of life. As a way of thinking it is ordinarily divided into these categories:

1. Metaphysics: thoughts about what the words *being, existence, unity, goodness, beauty,* etc. mean. It is thinking about what kind of reality or realities give unity and coherence to the world of change that we daily observe.
2. Logic: the study of the operations of the mind that are necessary for valid argumentation.
3. Epistemology: an investigation of what is "knowing," how we know, and what we know.
4. Ethics: philosophizing as a way of moral life. This is a threefold reasoning activity within free individuals. It is an activity that
   - arrives at some coherent meaning to life;
   - sets up a priority of values (i.e., what is worthwhile, good) based upon this meaning; and
   - acts according to these values.

The acclaimed or talented philosopher claims to present a much more profound, well-thought-out, and reasonable diagram for all or some of the above topics. Sometimes his or her approach is a vast interconnected system of philosophical thought. Some philosophers concentrate on only a small portion within one or the other of the above topics.

We who merely "philosophize" do so only at times. We are involved in various other life activities and hence do not use up that great amount of our energy only for the study of philosophy. Nevertheless, we are bound at times to philosophize in the same way that we are bound to think. We decide in either a clear or vague manner upon some purpose to our lives—even though some of us might conclude that our purpose is no purpose.

The study of philosophy is then an attempt to philosophize in a moral, formal, logically consistent, and deeper manner than that which we do day by day in our ordinary life situations. By formally trying to understand some of the thoughts of some of those philosophers whom the world has recognized as men and women of deep philosophical thought, we hope to formulate our own convictions about the issues that concern us most passionately in a clearer and more reasonably manner.

Approach the study of philosophy with these qualities:

1. Sincerity: try to find out what is really true. Try as much as possible to avoid "polemics." Try to be as intellectually honest as possible.
2. Tolerance: try to listen to or patiently read the arguments of other thinkers as you philosophize. Try to get rid of all personal prejudice. Try to understand as much as you can.
3. Benevolence and goodness: contact of the heart is a form of wisdom if it is open to great mental horizons. There is no wisdom without love.
4. Personal freedom and reflection: develop a sense of personal freedom in thought. That is, create a synthesis of self-knowledge, creative activity, and awareness of your feelings.

In our modern pluralistic society, the boundaries of philosophy are not fixed. Philosophy is the mental expression of freedom. It lives and thrives upon freedom of thought. Whoever learns to philosophize is a free human being—be he or she bodily in a prison, living in a totalitarian state, being watched in a fanatical religious state, and so on.

The ability to reflect is also one of the most beautiful powers of human existence. The philosopher takes comfort in using this power of reflection.

> Reflection is a domain reserved for human freedom. It goes against the compelling drive of nature. (C. G. Jung)

Read the ideas of a philosopher and then reflect upon whether they mirror your own personal experience. A life lived with reflection is often more important than a life lived only through books. If possible, read reflectively some original texts of the great authors. It is better to read less with reflection than to read more with no reflection. In this respect, the thought of A. Schopenhauer is illuminating:

> The constant streaming in of the thoughts of others must confine and suppress our own; and indeed in the long run paralyze the power of thought... When we read another person thinks for us; we merely repeat his mental process... So it comes about that if anyone spends almost the whole day in reading... he gradually loses the capacity of thinking... Experience of the world may be looked upon as a kind of text, to which reflection and knowledge form the commentary.

Philosophy, Faith, and Reason

Faith is a kind of knowledge of a truth or truths based on someone else's authority. It is accepting something as true because one wants to accept it as true! A person makes a choice to accept something as true because someone else told the person it is true. One simply believes the person is telling the truth.

We do this every day of our lives. We watch the news on TV. Something happens in Beijing, Africa, or South America. We have never been to Beijing, Africa, or those other places. We believe they exist as we trust the authority of the many geography books, magazines, newspapers, radio broadcasts, and TV reports about such countries. We could prove those cities and countries exist by going there. So this kind of faith is provable empirically. But until we do that, we make a choice to believe on the authority of someone else. Much of what we say we know is based on this kind of trusting faith.

If we philosophers wish to study the great masters of the past, we also must rely upon authority and faith. We *believe* that a number of books were written by certain authors. In reading specific ancient texts translated from many languages, we choose to accept that which we consider as the best authoritative text. For there is often controversy concerning the original writings. In summary, we study, read, and reflect within the stream of tradition and history—our knowledge of which relies upon authority.

However, there is another kind of faith that deals with truths that, although channeled to man through tradition and history, cannot be proven by reason. From this develops a personal religious faith. That is a conviction of knowing truths revealed to man by God or some far greater power than the limited logical reasoning function of man. The content of religious faith is not directly as religious beliefs a matter for philosophy. However, the validity of the experience has been of philosophical concern for centuries.

This kind of religious faith is a very problematic notion for philosophers, especially those who hold the view that any truth can only be attained and verified by logical empirical means. However, religious faith—presuming it deals with truth—is *alogical* or *beyond reason.* It does not begin, as does philosophy, by rationally inquiring into the existence of and the nature of first principles. Religious faith states that it is *already in possession* of the most basic principles concerning man, the world, and (depending on the religious faith) God—but by faith, not by empirical evidence. It uses more than sentences to express those truths. It uses rites and rituals, sacred actions, myths, and other activity forms.

However, some great religious faiths have developed reasonable philosophies to show that matters of belief are not irrational (though they be nonrational or transrational). There have been and are outstanding Jewish, Christian, Islamic, and Buddhist philosophers who contend that philosophy is also necessary to shed light on the deeper meanings inherent in their tenets of belief. Philosophy is also helpful in demonstrating that their beliefs are credible. Philosophy helps communicate their beliefs in a rational way to other thinking men and women.

Should we grant that **Truth** can be experienced and lived through religious faith, it still remains problematic rationally to decide which beliefs might stem from true "religiosity" and which ones might be sham truths resulting from fantastic manifestations, partial ideologies, pure fanaticism, the need for certain institutions to maintain their power, etc.

It is a matter for discussion whether philosophy should hold itself completely aloof from religion and restrict itself only to what can be known intellectually in the sense of critical reasoning.

Philosophy and Opinion

However, in normal pluralist philosophical discourse, it seems best for the most part to rely only upon reason as it flows from the functions of sensation and intellect. Otherwise, the argumentation between philosopher-believers and philosopher-nonbelievers tends to become sterile and emotionally charged. The point of C. J. Jung has merit:

> Religious experience is absolute. One cannot discuss the matter.
> One can only say that one has never had such an experience,
> and the opponent will say: I'm sorry about that, but I've had it!

Intuition and emotion—which are functions of faith knowledge—can become very subjective. However, these two functions cannot be entirely discounted in individual philosophizing.

Some philosophers philosophize within strictly logical thought constructs developed within a hermetically sealed universe, the structure of which is only the contingent and constantly changing. They dismiss other forms of thinking—such as "oceanic" thinking or "paradox" thinking—as incapable of being scientifically proven, perhaps naive, or at least outside the field of true philosophy. The data of modern physics would seem to indicate that it is unwise to dismiss outright these other forms of paradoxical thinking.

It is argued that in an apparently contingent and changing universe, this is all that can be expected. That means that one's first principles cannot be self-evident or absolute because they rest on the wave of change.

What seems to be the end result is a thought world of "opinions." That is, one holds a proposition to be true but with some fear that it might not be true, or that the quality of its truth is changing.

Other philosophers think that man is and can understand himself as existing *in* but *not totally* a part **of** such a *sealed-off* material universe.

These philosophers—be they Western or Eastern—think that man is a "transcendent" being and thus can discover unchangeable realities beyond the realm of the physically changing material environment. However, their propositions do not seem to be self-evident truths for all, or else all philosophers would easily intellectually accept them.

Opinion then, like faith, ultimately depends upon a choice. When all the evidence is studied, one chooses as (probably) true one philosophical proposition over many others. This often involves a concatenation of opinion/propositions, all of which are intrinsically connected with the others. A personal philosophical "worldview" then develops.

The above is a simplistic description of the philosophizing mental process. One's own life experience is a necessary ingredient to philosophizing. One's language, sex, cultural milieu, historical era, education, psychological makeup, life experiences, unconscious motivations, etc. influence the process and choice to a greater or lesser extent.

At times, the study of the many theories contained in philosophy may become exasperating. We begin to recognize the apparent contradictions within the thoughts of various philosophers. The different "schools" of philosophical thought can confuse us; they all, in their beginning stages, seem to be reasonable approaches to understanding philosophical issues. In later stages, the various viewpoints seem to contradict one another. The paradoxes are myriad. We begin to feel as if we are drowning in a swamp of confusing and murky ideas.

Nevertheless, within this maze of opinions, the serious philosopher tries to find his or her way by becoming as intelligent, understanding, free, and objective as possible in his or her attempt to reasonably discover the "truth" underlying the issue. Truth causes us to become free persons: *The truth will make you free!*

Chapter Two

The Beginnings

Western philosophy for the most part began in ancient Greece. From approximately the eleventh to the eighth century BC the peoples of Greece developed what we call Hellenic Life. The Greeks were called Hellenes. They were a people of mixed religious experiences. Belief in gods, ghosts, and demons was part of the everyday experiences of ordinary Greeks. Slowly a semicommon religion developed over centuries. Mystery religions played a part in the Greeks' religious experience. That is, rites were developed and ways of living evolved that stressed the never-ending cycle of birth and death as seen in nature. There was, however, a "saving" distinctive feature surrounding the meaning of the various mystery experiences. By means of these shared experiences, the initiates believed they could escape the cycle of birth and death and achieve unending life and power.

The gods and goddesses played another major role in public and private life. Of the major deities, *Zeus* was the chief god and father. He was the god of the sky, lightning, and thunder. *Hera* was his wife. *Poseidon* was the god of the seas and oceans. *Apollo* was the god of reason and music. He was the god of foretelling the future and poetry. One of his famous temples was at *Delphi*. *Athena* was the goddess of just war and wisdom. She was also the protector of Athens. Perhaps the wildest god was *Dionysus* or *Bacchus*. He was the god of wine and strong drink. Eventually, he evolved into a tamer god. Feasts were held in his honor during which plays were presented. This was the origin of drama and tragedy in literature.

For centuries, human beings' destinies and the events occurring in nature were explained as acts determined by the gods, who often acted on whims, made decisions out of anger or affection, and could be cajoled into granting favorable requests through human rites, prayers, and offerings. The Greek gods were immortal, but they were often viewed as very human with human strengths and weaknesses. A *mythological explanation* of the universe nourished human curiosity about the meaning and significance of the universe. A crude, simplistic, and embryonic scientific explanation was to be a development in later philosophy.

The Greeks became flourishing colonizers. First, traders traveled to many parts of the Mediterranean, then soldiers followed to protect the traders, and finally Greek citizens arrived to establish colonies. Many of the colonies developed into first-rate city-states. Greece had not been united as a single, independent, unified country. The ancient civilization was a loose cohesion of city-states. That is, each city-state was a small country in itself. Each had its own constitution. Often the forms of government varied. Some city-states were managed by "tyrants." Others, like Athens, evolved into democracies. It was against this background that Greek philosophy evolved.

Three of the most renowned of ancient classical Greek philosophers were Socrates, Plato, and Aristotle. The influence of these three thinkers is still being felt in philosophy. The center of the philosophical world and the civilization in which they lived was Athens. However, Western philosophy was not born in Athens. Philosophical speculation as we know it began among the Greek colonists in Asia Minor (Ionia) and southern Italy in the fifth and sixth centuries before Christ.

It is difficult to know exactly what these earliest philosophers said and what they actually meant. It is hard to know precisely what they may have meant in their teachings because we possess only fragments of their original writings. Extracts of their thoughts are mentioned in the writings of later authors who claimed to report accurately what these earlier philosophers had taught. Interpretations of modern philosophers regarding the meaning and importance of the thought of these early pre-Socratic philosophers vary. Some scholars have even suggested that Plato and Aristotle brought about a decline of philosophy if one were to compare the ideas of Plato and Aristotle with the alleged purer and more profound thought of the pre-Socratics.

Be that as it may, before this early beginning of pure philosophical speculation, Western philosophy was often a mixture of myth, mystery, fantasy, religion, and a few lucid intervals of purely logical reasoning. Religion, belief, and mythology served as the framework around which questions concerning the gods, nature, moral law, and the meaning of man's existence were framed. Man, to be sure, was believed to be something unique and special. Man was more than a mere animal. The early theologians and their followers emphasized that man's meaning and destiny was caught up in a process saturated with gods and goddesses, fiends and Furies, Fates and shadowy underworlds that were the abodes of the dead. The belief of the times professed that man could only experience life's meaning and fulfill life's obligations within the range allotted him by fate and the gods.

The pre-Socratic philosophers began *to divorce reason from faith.* They thus created an embryonic rational philosophical procedure in order to raise and answer questions about man and the universe. Reason, and not belief, was the vehicle of inquiry. The pre-Socratics provided the energizing stimulus of purely rational thought that over many centuries culminated in modern science. Moreover, without their initial reflections, there may not have been a Plato or an Aristotle, two of the greatest of early Greek philosophers.

Using reason as an instrument, these early philosophers were searching for a single unifying principle of all that exists. Moreover, they were searching for the principle or underling cause not in the doings of the gods, but in the natural events occurring in a nature that they could observe.

Ionians

The philosophers from Ionia (presently the western coastline of Turkey) framed questions and generated answers concerning the origins of the world. They especially struggled to fathom *what unifying "ageless" or "permanent" entity was both the substratum and also all pervading in the whole of reality.* They attempted to give answers by using their powers of observation and reason. They began to seek in a rational manner answers to the riddle of time-space-change-permanence-unity. It was their method of inquiry—divorced as it was from gods, semigods, mythology, and religion—that was most important and not necessarily the content of their conclusions.

Thales, who lived in the first quarter of the sixth century BC, maintained the principle of unity was water. Through his observations concerning the evaporation of water, rainfall, and the silting up process on the earth, he concluded that water was the original "stuff," matter, or source of all the other entities in the world. Water was the cause of all things.

Anaximander, who lived a little later than Thales, claimed the original unifying source was some amorphous "apeiron" (the infinite and boundless).

> Of those who say that it is one, moving, and infinite, Anaximander, son of Praxiades, a Milesian, the successor and pupil of Thales, said that the principle and element of existing things was the apeiron, being the first to introduce this name of the material principle. He says that is neither water nor any other of the so-called elements, but some other apeiron nature, from which come into being all the heavens and the worlds in them. And the source of coming-to-be for existing things is that into which destruction, too, happens "according to necessity; for they pay penalty and retribution to each other for their injustice according to the assessment of time." (*Simplicius*)

Anaximenes (611-546 BC) stated the source was air. He lived a little after Anaximander.

> He (Anaximander) left Anaximenes as his disciple and successor, who attributed all the causes of things to infinite air, and did not deny that there were gods, or pass them over in silence; yet he believed not the air was made by them, but that they arose from air. (*Augustine*)

Heraclitus came from Ephesus. He lived in the early fifth century BC. Heraclitus seemed to hold the opinion that the universe was eternal change. Fire was a prime source of reality. There is nothing permanent within his cosmos. Everything is eternally changing.

He, however, taught that there was **a** *purpose* and a *unifying ingredient* **within change. Wisdom, the goal of the philosopher, is to come to understand this unifying element and purpose within change. Moreover**

wisdom is *not gained by purely rational thought.* One is to "breathe in" the *Logos* (word, reason) to gain insight into the meaning of change. He taught that the wise man who is in contact with the Logos is able to experience the unity of all things.

What is the meaning of his use of the word *Logos*? Opinions vary. The word logos can variously mean speech, law, word, theorem, or reasoning. Ancient Greek poets described the process of thought as similar to "breathing in and out." Understanding was not just rational thinking based upon sense experience. A much deeper kind of understanding was to "breathe in" the truth in order to "breathe out" or speak the truth. The wise man is to breathe in the Logos. The word *Logos* as a way to ultimate Truth was to have a profound later influence upon Christian beliefs, theology, and philosophy.

Here are some of the reflections of Heraclitus.

Logos

Of the Logos, which is as I describe it, men always prove to be uncomprehending, both before they have heard it and when once they have heard it. For although all things happen according to this Logos, men are like people of no experience, even when they experience such words and deeds as I explain, when I distinguish each thing according to its constitution and declare how it is, but the rest of men fail to notice what they do after they wake up just as they forget what they do when asleep.

Listening not to me but to the Logos, it is wise to agree that all things are one.

Cosmos

The path up and down are one and the same.

In the same river we both step and do not step, we are and are not.

What is in opposition is in concert, and from what differs comes the most beautiful harmony.

Fire lives the death of earth, and air the death of fire; water
lives the death of air, earth that of water.

Pythagoras

Pythagoras is reported to have been born on Samos (a Greek island near
Ionia). However, he settled in Crotona in southern Italy. He lived in the
last quarter of the sixth century BC. He made important discoveries in
the field of mathematics and formed a community of philosophers who
lived together much like the Western monks in the Middle Ages. They
followed and lived an ascetical life. The Pythagoreans, or followers of
Pythagoras, placed a great deal of importance upon numbers as essential
elements making up the universe. The entire universe consisted of
relationships between numbers, intervals, and harmony. Numbers gave
harmony and order to the cosmos. All entities were but images of specific
numbers.

Man was a blend of soul (spirit) and body (matter). The soul was
more important than the body and on a far higher realm of existence.
The soul was the nonmaterial living force that gave life to the body.
However, the soul was in a sense imprisoned within the body. It was
being dragged down to inferior and lower forms of existence by the body.
The task of the true philosopher was to raise the soul above the body
and to become purified in mind and soul. Asceticism was a necessary
function of the true philosopher. Asceticism meant controlling the body.
It meant bringing the passions and emotions under control by arduous
labor, fasting, long periods of silence, and so on. Music also was a useful
instrument in this process of healing the soul and mind.

The ultimate purpose and goal of life was to achieve a harmonious
divinized state. However, this state was not something man could actually
conceive of. It was a state far removed from the soul-body condition
of the earthbound number being. One could talk about it. One could
try to imagine or picture this state as best as possible. The experience
of this state on the other hand was something far beyond the powers of
imagination to picture or beyond the powers of thought to conceive of.

They also believed in the transmigration of souls (reincarnation). If
one lived too sensual a life (a life of the *body*), one would later be reborn

in a lower form of life or even suffer horrible punishments in a hell after one has died.

There were many schools of thought that developed from Pythagoras. Some of them stressed the scientific and mathematical elements of his teachings. Others stressed the religious and mystical traits. Some elements of Pythagoreanism either directly or indirectly through later philosophers influenced Christianity—e.g., suppression of the bodily passions to free the soul—and have never died out.

Examples of the ideas of Pythagoras are

> The square of the hypotenuse of a right-angle triangle is equal to the sum of the squares on the sides enclosing the right angle. If we pay any attention to those who like to recount ancient history, we may find some of them referring this theorem to Pythagoras, and saying that he sacrificed an ox in honor of his discovery. (Proclus)
>
> On the subject of reincarnation, Xenophanes bears witness in an elegy which begins: "Now I will turn to another tale and show the way." What he says about Pythagoras runs thus: "Once they say that he was passing by when a puppy was being whipped, and he took pity and said: Stop, do not beat it; for it is the soul of a friend that I recognized when I heard it giving tongue." (Diogenes Laertius)
>
> Let the rules to be pondered be these:
>
> 1. When you are going out to a temple, worship first, and on your way, neither say nor do anything else connected with your daily life.
> 2. Sacrifice and worship without shoes on.
> 3. Follow the gods and restrain your tongue above all else.
> 4. Speak not of Pythagorean matters without light.
> 5. Abstain from beans.

The Eleatic School

Xenophanes

Xenophanes is the first representative of a school of philosophy developed in Elea in southern Italy. He was against the anthropomorphic conception of the gods as Homer and Hesiod has exhibited them to be. Xenophanes stated:

We possess only fragments of one of his poems.

> One God is greatest among the gods . . . he is not in his being at all like any being that is mortal nor is he like any being that can be conceived of.
>
> Homer and Hesiod ascribed to the gods whatever is infamy and reproach among men: theft and adultery and deceiving each other.
>
> Mortals suppose that the gods are born and have clothes and voices and shapes like their own.
>
> He sees as a whole, thinks as a whole, and hears as a whole.
>
> But without toil, he moves everything by the thought of his mind.
>
> Not from the beginning have the gods revealed all things to mortals, but by long seeking men find what is better.

Parmenides (540-470 BC)

Parmenides taught that all of reality is and can be only one. A world of change is logically impossible from his point of view. He also teaches inspiration and some kind of divine revelation, with its accompanying truth, is a path to knowledge distinct from common sense.

His basic idea is

- if change is from being, it already is.
- if change is from nothing, it is nothing.

> Only one way remains; that it is. To this way there are very many sign-posts: that being has no coming-into-being and no destruction, for it is whole of limb, without motion, and without end. And it never was, nor will be, because it is now, a whole all together, one, continuous.

Change can only therefore be a name but not a reality.

> Therefore all things that mortals have established, believing in their truth, are just a name: becoming and perishing, being and not-being, and change of position, alteration of bright color.

Being that permeates all other beings is unmoved and unchangeable. Aristotle utilized this theme would in his notions concerning the "unmoved mover." Parmenides was well aware of the discrepancy between his theory and man's ordinary daily experiences of changing things. He thus concluded that man's sense experiences are deceptive and lead to a false representation of true reality. Thus, empirical (sense) knowledge and knowledge gained by reason were strictly separated. True knowledge exists only within the one and unchangeable being itself. Plato drew upon these ideas of Parmenides.

Parmenides is considered a *monist* (**all is one**). Being and Truth are unchanging.

Pluralists

The philosophers who came after the Eleatics tried to show how change was possible. They are called pluralists because they tried to use a blend of many ultimate principles (*physeis*) to demonstrate the possibility of change. However, perhaps the word *pluralist* is not exactly correct as they also contended there was one principle of unity penetrating all change.

Empedocles (492-432 BC)

Empedocles held that the four most basic elements are air, water, earth, and fire. Change comes about by the intermixing of these elements.

For from these (elements)—water, earth, fire, and aid—come all things that were and are and will be; and trees spring up, and men and women, and beasts and birds and water-nurtured fish, and even the long-lived gods who are highest in honor. For these (elements) alone exist, but by running through one another they become different; to such a degree does mixing change them.

Hence there is no real destruction, but only a change of combinations of units. *The forces that cause the mixing of the basic elements are Love and Strife (Hate). There is an endless thesis and antithesis in the universe. Love will form harmony; but then hate will cause separation and destruction.*

And these (elements) never cease their continuous exchange, sometimes uniting under the influence of love, so that all become one, at other times again each moving apart through the hostile force of hate.

Observe her with your mind, and do not sit with wondering eyes! She (love) it is who is believed to be implanted in mortal limbs also; through her they think friendly thoughts and perform harmonious actions, calling her joy Aphrodite.

But in wrath they are all different in form and separate, while in (the reign of) love they come together and long for one another.

Surrounding and penetrating this intermixing fullness is God.

But he (God) is equal in all directions to himself and altogether eternal, a rounded sphere enjoying a circular solitude.

He believed in reincarnation and a kind of karma.

For by now I have been born as boy, girl, plant, bird, and dumb sea-fish. There is an oracle of necessity, an ancient decree of the gods, eternal, sealed fast with broad oaths, that when one of the divine spirits whose portion is long life sinfully stains his own limbs with bloodshed, and following hate has sworn a false oath—these must wander for thrice ten thousand seasons far from the company of the blessed, being born throughout the period into all kinds of mortal shapes, which exchange one hard way of life for another.

Anaxagoras (Fifth Century BC)

In a teaching that appears similar to that of Empedocles, Anaxagoras also saw change as a constant mingling of entities. The ultimate elements are indivisible and *imperishable seeds.* In everything there is a portion of all other existing things. It is the preponderance of seeds that causes diversity.

But what causes the motion and direction of these seeds? Anaxagoras stated it was **"Nous"** or *Mind.* **It was Mind that caused order and physical laws in the universe.**

> In everything there is a portion of everything except Mind; and some things contain Mind also.

> Other things all contain a part of everything, but Mind is infinite and self-ruling, and is mixed with no Thing, but is alone by itself.

> And when Mind began the motion, there was a separating off from all that was being moved; and all that Mind set in motion was separated (internally); and as things were moving and separating off (internally), the revolution greatly increased this (internal) separation.

He appealed both to reason and to inspiration, insight, or revelation to persuade others of his teachings. Reason, however, had its limits.

> Through the weakness of the sense-perceptions, we cannot judge truth.

Democritus (460-379 BC)

Democritus is included in the list of pre-Socratic philosophers, although he was a younger contemporary of Socrates. Hence, he might have had to deal with the problems surrounding knowledge and ethical conduct in a more complex manner than the philosophers who went before him.

Democritus held that it is impossible to divide things to infinity. He held a teaching called *atomism*. That is, the universe is made up of countless atoms in perpetual motion. Atoms were of all sizes and shapes. They fell endlessly into a void. This void was also something, a reality in itself. By crashing together, the atoms caused the universe and endless change. Knowledge is not of any lasting truth or accuracy, but it is only relative because it always depends upon the changing condition of the body (atoms).

> Sweet exists by convention, bitter by convention, color by convention; atoms and void (alone) exist in reality . . . we know nothing accurately in reality, but (only) as it changes according to bodily condition, and the constitution of those things that flow upon (the body) and impinge upon it.

He also posited limits to empirical knowledge. When rational knowledge has reached its furthest limits, another kind of knowledge takes over.

> There are two sorts of knowledge, one genuine, one bastard (or "obscure"). To the latter belong all the following: sight, hearing, smell, taste, touch. The real is separated from this. When the bastard can do no more—neither see more minutely, nor hear, nor smell, nor taste, nor perceive by touch—and a finer investigation is needed, then the genuine comes in as having a tool for distinguishing more finely.

He developed ethical observations that were to have long-lasting influence. In future centuries, many philosophers adhered to these principles. Here are some examples:

It is right that men should value the soul rather than the body; for perfection of soul corrects the inferiority of the body, but physical strength without intelligence does nothing to improve the mind.

He who chooses the advantages of the soul chooses things more divine, but he who chooses those of the body, chooses things human.

Men find happiness neither by means of the body nor through possessions, but through uprightness and wisdom.

Refrain from crimes not through fear but through duty.

Magnanimity consists in enduring tactlessness with mildness.

One should emulate the deeds and actions of virtue, not the words.

It is better to examine one's own faults than those of others.

The enmity of relatives is much worse than that of strangers.

Be not suspicious towards all, but be cautious and firm.

To make money is not without use, but if it comes from wrong-doing, nothing is worse.

The cause of error is ignorance of the better.

Life is not worth living for the man who has not even one good friend.

Many avoid their friends when they fall from wealth to poverty.

The man who loves nobody is, I think, loved by no one.

Medicine heals diseases of the body, wisdom frees the soul from passions.

Man is a universe in little (microcosm).

The excessive accumulation of wealth for one's children is an excuse for covetousness, which thus displays its peculiar feature.

Freedom of speech is the sign of freedom, but the danger lies in discerning the right occasion.

To the wise man, the whole earth is open; for the native land of a good soul is the whole world.

Democritus held that the goal of man's ethical striving was to achieve serenity and harmony within the human soul. Man's reason can accomplish this by holding on to a middle path. That means one should not go to extremes in seeking sense pleasure. Spiritual values are more important.

The Sophists

We have no original works from this class of educator philosophers. The Sophists seemed to have been professional educators who taught for a price. This was a change in the Greek educational practice. The older tradition of leaving the education of one's offspring to members of the family, relatives, or patrons seemed to have had its disadvantages. Therefore a class of professional teachers, the Sophists, developed.

The name *Sophist* comes from a Greek word that originally meant "a wise man." The Sophists, however, for the most part seemed to have taught that certitude of any truth was impossible to attain. They thought that the best one could do was to learn the art of public speaking, debating, and rhetoric. This was the proper preparation for a good career within Greek society. They contended that they could impart this preparation to their students. Some Sophists were eager to teach their students how to make the better cause seem worse, and the worse cause see to be the better one. In time, argument for its own sake was the most important thrut of education. Sophistry took on the negative meaning of "quibbling" for its own sake without any regard for the lighting up of permanent Truth.

The Sophists apparently held that the purpose of education was to train one to achieve success "in the world" in a humane sense. Hence they stressed, among other things, rhetoric and oratory (public speaking) with that goal in mind. Persuasion was often more important than knowledge. Some of the Sophists were skeptics concerning the gods and men's relationship to the gods or what bearing the gods, if they existed, might have on a successful life.

One Sophist, Protagoras, is reported to have said,

> Man is the measure of all things, of the things that are, that
> they are, of the things that are not, that they are not.

That is, human beings only judge all of nature and the moral law through our own *subjective* experiences. There is nothing "out there" in nature by which we make moral decisions.

Lycophron taught the idea that law is a social contract or a covenant made up for the mutual protection of all citizens. This theme was to arise once again centuries later in the writings of Thomas Hobbes, a British philosopher of the early modern era.

Hippias, in the words of Plato, taught that law tyrannizes people and forces them to do things against their nature. Thrasymachus, on the other hand, sees law as an instrument of the mighty to exploit and oppress the weak. Critias sees religion as an invention to prevent evildoers from doing evil because of their fear of the wrath of the gods.

We do not know all of the original philosophical platforms of the Sophists. They did stress, however, the relativity of knowledge. That is, there can be no certitude as regards to what is true. They also extended this to ethics or moral law. That is, there can be no certitude concerning which human actions are right and which are wrong. It all depends on the individual experiences of individuals and how they make moral judgments by way of these fleeting experiences.

Significance of the Pre-Socratics

These very early philosophers opened the doors to philosophical problems that later philosophers were to struggle with for centuries. One of the most basic problems, which is basic to all others, is the problem of the "one" and the "many." That is, is there only one unifying principle for all of reality or is all of reality only a never-ending process of change.

The solution to this problem is still important, for example, in the area of *ethics* **or** *morality.* Is there some basic moral law that is unchanging? Is all of morality only the reflection of constant change with no claim to permanent validity?

Do the *sciences* have any legitimate claim to knowing "the truth" if the foundation of their knowledge rests upon an endless, impermanent process of change. Or are there some fixed and permanent laws of nature that express themselves in change, but are themselves unchangeable? If such laws exist, where are they?

What is the **value of knowledge?** Is there really **any** knowledge of the truth? The pre-Socratics introduced Western philosophy into a chaotic and paradoxical philosophical world that on the one hand was a world of permanence, absolute truth, spirit, and reason, and on the other hand was a world of materialism, skepticism, relativism, and nihilism. It would be up to future philosophers to attempt to bring order out of this chaos.

Chapter Three

Socrates

Socrates lived in the fifth century BC. The most important source of our knowledge of the teachings of Socrates is contained in the dialogues of his pupil, Plato. He was a man who was not physically handsome. He lived through a period when Athens had lost a long civil war with Sparta. He thus lived through a period of defeat in war, the rise of oligarchy, and the reestablishment of democracy in Athens. He apparently wrote nothing. We know about him and his thought only through later philosophers, especially Plato. In all probability, this thought is already colored by Plato and others. It is impossible to know exactly what Socrates taught.

Socrates was a veteran who had served in the Athenian citizen army. He had always done his duty to the state. He was not an "armchair" philosopher. He put into practice what he taught. He was an obedient citizen. It was only when the state—whether it was the democratic state or the oligarchical state—wished him to obey an immoral command (law) that he refused. This happened on several occasions during his lifetime.

Socrates had a belief that a "special voice" was assisting him and urging him to discuss with those who would listen to him. He tried to get people to "examine" their lives, to reflect upon goodness, truth, beauty, the meaning of a good life, and virtue. He was obsessed with the sentence etched into Apollo's famous temple at Delphi: *Know Your Self.*

He believed that true wisdom, insight, and happiness within the self and its powers of reason. One must search within the self to discover true understanding of what a good life really is and then go on to live it. He thought that the evil actions of men were caused by their own ignorance of what was good. Therefore, it was necessary for a person to discover and live by truth in order to live a good life.

Hence, knowing and understanding what was good and decent was a first step. *One could not do what one did not know!* The method that he used to achieve this end was question, answer, analysis, further questions, and further analysis until the truth (based on true definitions) was reached. The negative route of this method was to force the person with whom he was arguing into a corner. Socrates would question unremittingly each theory that an opponent would produce until a stage was reached when one had to admit total ignorance. Then one could proceed along positive lines to build up a clearer and more reasonable viewpoint on such subjects as what is piety, what is loyalty, what is justice, what is love, etc. Socrates was constantly searching for adequate and lucid definitions of specific virtues that led to a good and ethically harmonious life.

This theory was naturally based on the assumed principle that a person—by using his or her reason—can come to a clear understanding of unchanging and ultimate definitions that conform to some "outside" reality.

To practice his method, he would walk about the city of Athens and hold discussions with individuals or groups of people (often young people) who were concerned with moral philosophy. He did not seem to be interested in the metaphysical or cosmological speculations of his predecessors. He was interested in philosophy only to the extent that it would help lead a person to moral perfection in his or her individual life. This in turn would be a help to bring about a moral society. Social evils would be overcome by first rooting out one's personal faults based upon ignorance.

Socrates often used irony. That is, Socrates would claim that he was quite ignorant concerning the questions he was discussing. He condescended to his opponent's apparent "deeper" knowledge of the matter under discussion. He would then commence to ask questions of his opponent and make a fool of him by leading the person to demonstrate and accept his own ignorance of the matter.

Socrates was fond of claiming that he himself "knew nothing." However, because he knew he knew nothing, he claimed he knew more than those who thought they knew a lot, but in actuality knew nothing.

Socrates believed that his method was not unlike that of a midwife. He was only helping his opponent perceive the truth himself. Socrates was not teaching a truth; he was merely using a method to assist others to come to knowledge of the truth themselves. The **Socratic method** is still a useful tool in logical argumentation.

Socrates made frequent references to a **"divine voice"** that often inspired him about which direction to go in critical moments of his life. Socrates possessed a belief in God (gods?) and seemed certain of the immortality of his soul.

He so believed in what he was doing—i.e., trying to bring others to a knowledge of the good—that he was brought to trial by politicians and others when he was an old man. He was accused of denying the gods and corrupting the youth of the city. He was condemned to death and sentenced to take poison.

His life had a tremendous effect on many philosophers. Among them was Plato. Plato was a disciple of Socrates for about seven years. Plato tried to pass on the thought of Socrates through his own writings.

Three writings of Plato—the *Apology, Crito,* and *Phaedo*—seem to reflect somewhat accurately the genuine thought and manner of speech of Socrates.

The *Apology* (Defense) was the defense that Socrates himself made before the court that was trying him. In the *Apology*, Socrates describes his manner of life and his philosophical convictions most clearly. He felt that he was being driven by a godlike impulse or divine voice. He tried to care for everyone. He was willing to give up his life to achieve his goal, which was to awaken men to a higher truth by which they could mold for themselves a good life. Nothing else was important.

Chapter Four

Plato (427-348 BC)

Plato was born in Athens in 427 BC. He came from an influential and wealthy parentage. He had a good education as he was growing up. When he was younger, Plato was enthusiastic about poetry. Probably due to the influences of his family, Plato was also interested in politics and how to better political situations. Many of his uncles were involved in politics. The family expected him to go into politics also.

In one of his letters, Plato talks about how, in his younger years, he was enthusiastic about entering politics as soon as he was old enough. It was a time of revolution in Athens. Plato began to observe how the new rulers with their new constitution acted. They had promised a new and just beginning in Athenian society. But then he observed how they acted—that is, not at all justly. They tried to persuade Socrates to vote along with them in an unfair conviction of a man opposed to their views. Socrates would not go along with them because he was convinced that their machinations were unjust. Yet when another revolution occurred and the man whom Socrates was instrumental in keeping alive came to power, he was one of the group who ultimately condemned Socrates to death. It was then that Plato became disenchanted with politicians and politics.

He saw how much evil politicians could do—both those who ruled under the oligarchy and those who ruled under a democracy. *He came to the conclusion that evil men were the cause of an evil form of government. He turned to philosophy in hopes of influencing men to be good men and thus good and honest politicians. In this way, a good and just society would evolve.*

When he was about twenty years old, he met Socrates. This meeting created a dramatic change in Plato's interests. He became engrossed in the pursuit of wisdom or philosophy. Plato became a fervent disciple of Socrates and his greatest exponent after Socrates had died.

After the death of Socrates, Plato continued his studies in philosophy. He traveled to Egypt, Asia Minor, and Sicily. He studied the teachings of the Pythagoreans in Italy.

Plato made three trips to Sicily. Plato made an attempt to put his philosophical and political theories into practice. He was given the chance to try out his ideas concerning good government. In Syracuse in Italy, he tried to assist in the training of a new ruler, Dionysius II. He did this at the request of his friend, a man named Dion, who was related to Dionysius II. Plato was a failure in his mission. He tried to counsel, instruct, and teach two rulers—the older and younger Dionysius—on how to govern wisely. Plato's attempts floundered. He was arrested and made a slave for a while.

After having been ransomed by a friend, Plato returned to Greece. He founded his own school of philosophy called the *Academy* in 385 BC. In a sense, this might be called the first university in Europe. It attracted many scholars and teachers to Athens. Science, mathematics, law, and philosophy were taught in rigorous form in the Academy. It became the most prestigious institution of its time. It lasted for nine hundred years.

Plato taught and wrote until he was eighty years old.

Although there are some extant letters written by Plato, the Dialogues (i.e., conversations about philosophical themes) are the most important of his written works. In them, he expresses his views on many topics in philosophy. The Dialogues are conversational philosophical discussions. Plato often uses the names of familiar characters, figures known to the Athenians of that time, in his dialogues.

Plato considered written words to be inferior to spoken words. Actual conversation and discussion, he contended, was the best way to bring about deeper insights into the meaning of wisdom. He stated that the genuine method of teaching philosophy evolves almost spontaneously in the spoken word as if the words were kindled by a spark or light within the soul. Nevertheless, the written word was second best for those who would not have the chance to discuss with him personally.

The written works are the only original source we have of Plato's thought. The written words of Plato, however, are, in comparison to his living words, rather inferior and imperfect attempts to formulate in some measure the insights he was experiencing in his philosophical quest. Often he could not really express his insights clearly and comprehensively. His words then often seemed like poetry. They thus are open to many interpretations. They are descriptions of what he thought rather than precisely formed definitive ideas or concepts.

Plato also used myths and allegories in his writings. That is, he used a type of fantastic story, sometimes rooted far back in Greek history, to teach a deeper meaning than that which he was able to express in a literal or factual sense.

Socrates is a prominent character in Plato's dialogues. However, Socrates is often only a "mouthpiece" for the thoughts of Plato. Socrates undoubtedly taught many things attributed to him in some of Plato's dialogues. Nevertheless, so many of his views have been interpreted, transformed, and expanded by Plato in the dialogues, that it becomes often impossible to know what is the genuine thought of Socrates and what is an embellished viewpoint offered by Plato.

The method that Plato follows in his dialogues in his search for wisdom (virtue) is adopted from the Sophists and especially from Socrates. It is *dialectics*. That is, the ideas one has about a point in philosophical discussion are torn apart and then analyzed meticulously until one has a clear definition of whatever it is that one is discussing. *For Plato, the clear definition took on the meaning of a clear apprehension of reality or of being itself. Dialectics became thus a form of metaphysical inquiry. The dialogue is a perfect vehicle to apply this method.*

Teachings

Plato's thought is bound up with his times. He sometimes was against certain types of thinking and at other times developed further the thought of others.

His foremost foes were the Sophists. Plato considered it a fundamental error to hold that man was the measure of all reality. He thought this form of relativism would lead to chaos and the destruction of all theories of certain knowledge. Furthermore, such a principle would be the ruin of any permanent foundations for ethical and moral life. Nevertheless,

Plato held some ideas in common with the Sophists. Plato employed the dialectical method as did the Sophists. Plato was mistrustful of the "wisdom" of the common man, as were the Sophists. Plato was mistrustful of putting too much truth value into sense experience, as were the Sophists.

Plato separated himself nevertheless from the Sophists and several of the pre-Socratic philosophers in that he was convinced that a stable foundation for permanent and unchangeable truth both existed and could be known. It was this eternal and unchangeable truth that was the fountainhead of what truth value there was in changeable and impermanent reality. *Therefore, man was not the measure of all things; rather, man could discover and know the measure of all things.*

Plato, like Socrates, was convinced that many of the Sophists were in error when they taught and emphasized that there was no stable rational basis for *ethical judgments.* Plato was convinced that the world of moral values and norms was *not* just a world of ever-changing viewpoints and attitudes founded upon and produced by the ever-changing standpoints of societies and cultures. He understood where such a world of moral and ethical relativism would lead. That is, such a conviction would ultimately lead to political and moral chaos or to a social management based on the principle that *might makes right!*

To refute the Sophists, however, Plato needed to erect a rational philosophical structure by which he would have a firm foundation to explain what the world of appearances was and what relationship these appearances and phenomena had to truth. Plato brought together in a synthesis the conflicting worlds of Parmenides and Heraclitus. That is, Plato tried to offer a solution to the apparent contradiction between the "one" and the "many." The world of constant change is real, but the world of unchangeableness was more real. In fact, this world of unchangeableness is the reason why there can be a world of change.

The creative inspiration that Plato first conceived of and then developed was his *theory of ideas* or *theory of forms.* **That is, ideas in themselves existed as immaterial, eternal, and unchangeable beings or entities.** Ideas are the archetypes and the molds that *form* all of the objects of the visible world. These ideas or forms have an *objective* reality. That is, they are *not* the product of man's consciousness and they are not thoughts produced by man. They are rather that which man *can become conscious of.* They exist *before* man can think about them. Plato's position can be described as *objective idealism.*

In essence, Plato was convinced of the existence of two spheres or worlds of reality. The one, the world that we sense is always fluctuating, shifting, inconstant, and mutable—the world of Heraclitus, Democritus, and others. The other, the world of pure ideas, is forever established, immutable, constant, and eternal—similar to the view of Parmenides. Relying upon his two-world-theory, Plato asserted that the material world of change was thoroughly dependent both *ethically and ontologically* upon the world of eternal ideas. *The inferior or lower world of phenomena, change, and fluctuating sensation derived its being and existence from the world of ideas.* With this theory, Plato was able to harmonize the apparent paradox between the viewpoints of Parmenides and Heraclitus. From Plato's standpoint, both Parmenides and Heraclitus were correct if they were correctly interpreted. Plato had a solution for the question as to whether all of reality was "one" or "many." The solution was . . . *it depends!* That is, it depends on what sphere of reality one was reflecting upon. If one is considering the sphere of immutable and eternal ideas, there is a certain unity. If is one is considering the visible and changeable sphere of reality, there is definitely multiplicity.

Plato thought that all of the sensible objects that we become aware of already share in the idea of what it is. That is, a book is a book because it shares in the idea (or definition) of a book. A dog is a dog because it shares in the idea of what a dog essentially is. We could perhaps make up words to characterize these ideas. For example, Plato asserts that "book-ness," "dog-ness," "table-ness," and so on are real entities existing apart from individual and concrete books, dogs, or tables.

Plato thought that the individual material object outside of our minds is the instrument and impetus whereby a concept is formed in the mind (soul). The outside object is, however, *not the true cause* of the concept or idea in the mind. The true cause is a deeper knowledge that a soul possessed *before* it was born into the material world joined to a body. That is, the soul in this life remembers what it had intellectually seen and understood in a previous "nonbodily" life. Knowledge is therefore in reality a **remembering. It is in the final process an "intuition." That is, one is ultimately immediately aware of the "idea"** as such. **The truth is already within the human soul. One needs only to become aware of it, or to "intuit" it, to grasp it directly without the use of any intermediary entity.**

Plato contended that the ideas we have in our minds are true ideas only if they share in some way in the ideas of the metaphysical (i.e., beyond and transcending the physical) universe of *ideas.* **As mentioned, material objects are also real only** *because* they share in the metaphysical world of ideas. A pen is a pen because it has the "essence" of pen-ness. A man has the essence of "human," a horse has the essence of "horse-ness," and so forth. **Plato had never explained clearly** *how* **a concrete object could share in the total essence of the idea.** This was to be a problem for one of his great students, Aristotle.

In other words, the definition of something is a reality in the world of ideas (forms). It is not just something that we make up in our minds. In fact, we possess a true definition of something in our minds if we *mentally* share in the *idea itself* (existing in the world of ideas) of whatever we are perceiving.

According to Plato, then, true knowledge within a time and space dimension takes place in the mind (in the soul), but it begins in the body. To explain Plato's thought in more modern terms, knowledge begins with outside stimuli causing sensations of color, sound, etc. in the body. The nerve impulses relay these to the brain. The brain puts all of the stimuli in order very quickly, and a picture is formed in the brain. *According to Plato, the soul then remembers, and this remembering is in the form of an abstraction or idea.* The picture is the impetus whereby a concept (idea) comes to be in the soul.

Plato teaches that these mental nonmaterial images (concepts) can be combined with other mental images to form judgments. If these judgments conform to the truth reality (which is outside of the individual mind and in the world of ideas), then true knowledge occurs.

However, if the knowledge stops at the material object, it remains confused, imperfect, incomplete, and shaky. If one proceeds from the material plane and goes ever higher in the mind to the world of ideas, then a much fuller, more perfect, and truer level of knowledge is reached.

It is only *true* knowledge that brings about wisdom in human beings. Plato thought that this was what philosophy was all about—to go ever higher with the mind and soul into the world of ideas.

For he thought, like Socrates, that if a man knew the truth, he (or she) would live the truth. If a man knew really what was good, he would live a good life. If he knew really what love was, he would love other human beings, etc. *The evil actions that men do stem from ignorance.* They do evil because they think that such actions will bring them some good and thus bring about happiness. They think that evil will bring about true happiness. Plato claimed this was only ignorance due to lack of true knowledge of what the "Good" is. *Knowledge is firmly connected with ethics.*

Plato thought that the more one's soul is exposed to and shares in the world of ideas, the clearer and more certain is the grasp of truth. There is a shadowy and inconstant kind of truth grasped in the world of sensation and phenomena. However, the truth is *not* **absolutely certain.** *It rests upon temporary conviction, belief, or opinion.* **One can change one's mind about its verity or accuracy.**

A life of philosophizing is then also a life leading to a type of immortality. Plato's philosophical theories about the possibility of being untied to the Good and to the world of eternal ideas, the place of remembering, the importance of reincarnation had already taken root in Greek consciousness in a more religious form. That is, the "mystery cults and beliefs" had already been widespread.

These were rites and beliefs that man could escape the many cycles of rebirth and also achieve a blissful immortality in another dimension of reality after leaving the body. One of the more widespread and significant mystery cults was the Orphic Mysteries. Orpheus was a person who supposedly descended into the underworld, the world of the souls who had left their bodies at death. He went there to bring back one particular soul. In the myths concerning Orpheus and Orphic cosmology runs the idea that mortal men are a hybrid of the gods and mortals. Man is thus divine and not divine at the same time under different aspects. The soul, the divine spark, is reborn. The body, the mortal segment, returns to dust.

The soul has a chance by living a religiously virtuous life, by practicing certain kinds of asceticism (such as not eating meat), by participating in certain kinds of religious rites, to achieve a state of being in which the cycle of rebirth is broken. The soul is then saved eternally.

For Plato, the religious elements were philosophically purified, so to speak. Salvation meant a soul connection with Truth within the world of ideas.

The understanding of virtue and its attainment through a dialectical, intellectual, and contemplative process substituted for the religious rites of the mystery religions. The body remained still a type of prison for the soul. The godlike soul had already intellectually communicated with the absolute Truth before its having been incarnated in the body. There is therefore a quasidivine knowledge within the soul, although for many it is neither known nor acknowledged. *To acknowledge the existence and importance of the soul is a first step in ultimately "remembering" what the soul really knows.* The religious mysteries in Plato have become philosophical mysteries.

Anthropologically, Plato sees the human being as a composition of various elements. Among these are the following:

- The Soul (immortal): a spiritual element which is the foundation and substance of the human personality.
- The Body (mortal): the material element which has life through the union with the soul.

The soul has various drives, functions, or powers. They exist at various levels of the soul. The highest and purest function is *reason,* which can be almost divine. Another drive within the soul—whether because the soul is incarnated in the body, or whether the very nature of the soul is thus— is the *irrational* element of the soul. These are drives that make man akin to other animals. Some of these drives can be controlled by reason. They are the *irascible drives,* the feelings that demand courage and discipline to keep under control. Other drives are more difficult to be subjected to reason. These are the *concupiscible appetites* and *passions* that cry out mercilessly for satisfaction.

Linked to the three parts or drives of the soul are the predominant virtues. Virtues are acquired aids to create a balance and equilibrium between soul and body. *Wisdom* is the virtue cooperating with reason. *Fortitude* assists in keeping the irascible drives in check. *Temperance* cools the inflamed concupiscible appetites. *Justice* affects all parts of the soul and keeps them in harmony. Later, these were called the four cardinal or "hinge" virtues. All other virtues that man can learn and acquire "hinge" upon these four.

That the soul is *immortal* and spiritual is an essential element of Plato's metaphysics and epistemology.

> Thus the soul, since it is immortal and has been born many times, and has seen all things both here and in the other world, has learned everything that is. So we need not be surprised if it can recall the knowledge of virtue or anything else which, as we see, it once possessed. (*Meno*)

Moreover Plato asserted that "like can be known from like." That is, the soul knows pure being by grasping ideas in the world of ideas. In order to do this, the soul itself must be pure or nonmaterial. Hence it is not subject to death. As Plato states in the *Phaido*,

> The soul is most akin to the divine, the immortal, the reasonable, to that which cannot be extinguished.

A central point in the philosophy of Plato is the idea of the Good. Trying to discover what is "good" was the chief search for Socrates also. The "Good" holds a unique position in the thought of Plato. The "Good" is both the goal of philosophizing, and it is also at the root of all other ideas in the world of ideas. It is the light in and through which man understands all of reality. Plato compares the "Good" to the sun. Things become visible because of the sunlight. But they are also nourished and grow because of the sun. Plato thought analogously that all permanent realities (i.e., ideas) and all impermanent objects are impregnated with the "Good" and maintain their existence through the "Good." *Why that must be was not a question for Plato.*

It is man's immortal soul that has clearly comprehended the fullness of the "Good" before it had become incorporated or incarnated within a body. This proposition and suggestion of Plato is an intrinsic element within the science of ethics and morality. The goal and purpose of man is to achieve knowledge of the Good by an elevation of the soul into the realm of eternal ideas and thus once again enjoy the clarity of grasping all that is Good. The Body and material sensations are like chains and fetters that hold the soul back from this entrance into the eternal dimension.

A life of virtue is a condition of the soul that is close to reaching a union of the soul and the "Good." As visible things are images of the unseen eternal ideas, they can be a help in the flight into the unseen realm. Music and art are important in this respect. Virtue is ultimately, however, grounded upon immediate and clear insight into what is "Good." Plato thought that virtue could be known and learned. That is the purpose of philosophy. To become virtuous is to become wise.

Hence the predominance of reason is the guiding influence determining the good life. Reason recalls man to his real origins. Reason assists man to live through time into eternity. The supreme goal of human life and human aspirations is to totally transcend or go beyond the sensible world.

Politics—Society

Plato had always been interested in politics. Plato stressed repeatedly the idea that man is a social being. To be a good citizen in the fullest sense of the word is a goal of education (attaining wisdom). Everyone should be properly educated so that his or her talents can be developed and be a source of personal wisdom and satisfaction in addition to helping society. Women should be given the same education as men. Thus the goal and ideal of the state is to rule and educate so wisely so that each citizen would have the opportunity to develop wisely his or her potential.

Plato described the perfect state as one ruled by "wise" (philosopher) rulers (wise politicians). Philosophy must be an element of their education. They would be so wise that many laws would not be necessary. For once there is law, there can be inflexibility. Inflexibility leads to stagnation and acts of injustice toward individuals who do not "fit" into the legal structure. Plato thought that laws were only "second best" means of governing. The first and best form of government was one in which wise rulers governed.

Plato thought that there should be a hierarchy in this utopian society. There would be rulers, soldiers, merchants, ordinary people, etc. Everyone would have a place, be happy, and be able to develop along the lines of his or her abilities. Everyone would be given the chance to be happy. However, since it seemed impossible that such an ideal state (i.e., one in which wise rulers were always available) would ever come into being, Plato later in his life taught that just laws must be a part of a just society. These ideas are expounded in two major works of Plato. The works are called *The Republic* and *Laws.*

In summary, Plato thought that men and women do live in a world of change. A man or woman is born, changes, becomes old, and dies. But still this transient man or woman can also share in the world of permanence, unchangeableness, and immortality by obtaining wisdom. To seek true knowledge (wisdom) is the true meaning of life. To know the Good is to be good. Man is a mixture of the eternal (the soul) and the temporal (the body). The soul will never cease to exist. The body will.

If a man or woman lives a *good life,* this will affect other men and women in the society. A *good* society, a *good* government, is made up of *good* men and women. *There is a harmonious interacting between good men and women and society's ruling justly and wisely.*

The goal of the individual man or woman is to reach absolute enlightenment by possessing knowledge of eternal and unchangeable ideas.

These ideas are at the very core of a Western thought process that has stressed universal values and the universal good. This is not to say that every Westerner accepts the above description in exactly the same way. There have been countless variations of and solutions to the philosophical questions that Plato posed and tried to answer. However, his theories have molded considerably the outlook of Western thought.

CHAPTER FIVE

Aristotle

Aristotle was the most brilliant student of Plato. Aristotle (384-322 BC), born in the Ionian colony of Stagira in northern Greece, was the son of a physician to the Macedonian ruler. At eighteen, he entered Plato's Academy in Athens, where he remained for two decades until Plato's death. He then taught outside Athens for a dozen years, including three as tutor to the young prince who later became known as Alexander the Great. In 335, Aristotle came back to Athens and founded his own school, called the Lyceum, where he did his most fruitful teaching and research. When Alexander the Great died in 323, an outbreak of anti-Macedonian feeling swept Athens, and Aristotle went to the city of Chalcis. "Lest," he reportedly said, "the Athenians should sin twice against philosophy."

His school of thought was called the "peripatetic" school. Peripatetic comes from a Greek word "to walk." Aristotle used to lecture and teach his students while he and they were walking.

Aristotle was interested in all facets of knowledge. He was particularly keen on observation, experiment, and research. His Lyceum had a library filled with manuscripts of as many ancient thinkers as he could get his hands on, other research materials, and a "lab" for studies in botany and zoology. He encouraged his students to research, to test, and to evaluate whatever opinions they held in science or philosophy as much as possible.

Although Aristotle probably wrote some dialogues, they are no longer extant. The writings we do have by him or by way of his students are much "drier" than the *Dialogues* of Plato. These writings are in a prose style—very exact in the use and meaning of words. Aristotle was a "common-sense" philosopher. He tried to harmonize the typical "down-to-earth" way we view things with the more abstract way one "philosophizes" about reality. Aristotle saw more of *reality* and *truth* in the individual things in the universe than Plato did.

Aristotle was a great "systematizer." He was interested in *order* and classification. He was interested in empirical research. His own advances in the knowledge of philosophy began with his orderly insights into the thought of philosophers before and during his time. He would correct their errors, as he saw them, stress the true points of view that they offered, and then he would synthesize all within his own universal system of knowledge.

Many minds throughout the centuries agree that Aristotle's intellectual and philosophical achievements were of enormous greatness. He—last year, yesterday, position—sitting, action—to run, state—shod, affection (receptive of some action or stimulus)—to be lanced.

Aristotle thought that these categories were first in the things themselves. They existed in the objects outside of our minds, and we could come to know them. This was a very down-to-earth and common-sense approach to reality. It is termed *Realism*. Someone, for example, examining a book on a desk can say it is a substance (a book), it is eight inches long and six inches wide (quantity), it is white and black (quality), it is mine (relation), it is on the desk (place), it is there now (time), it is flat on the desk (position), and it is being touched by me (affection).

These simple concepts expressed in words are joined together in sentences. The joining together of words is called judgments and make up true or false sentences or *propositions*.

Aristotle developed rules by which the binding together of groups of sentences would lead to conclusions. The joining of *two* judgmental sentences could lead to a *third* judgmental sentence. The process was called a *syllogism*. In its simplest form Aristotle states,

> If A is predicated of all B, and B of all C, A must be predicated
> of all C. (Prior Analytics)
> A classical example of a syllogism is:
>   (A)   (B)

All men are mortal
  (C)   (B)
Socrates is a man
  (C)   (B)
(Therefore) Socrates is mortal.

The first two sentences, or propositions, are termed *premises*. The last proposition is the conclusion. The key word "mortal" (man) is termed the *middle term*. That is, it is a term *common* to both premises if used in the correct order.

There are many forms of the syllogism. They are studied in logic courses. A string of syllogisms can make up a proof for an argument. The method used is a *deductive* method. That means one goes from what is *generally known* to conclusions about a *particular* thing. An unanswered question might be: How does one know that the generally known propositions are true? It would seem they are either known in themselves as self-evident, by belief in some authority (which is not certain knowledge—all of the authorities might err), or from *experience* whereby one must rely upon the counterpart to the deductive method—namely, *induction.*

Importantly, moreover both in his discourses on logic and in his philosophical treatises, especially when he treats of metaphysics, he founded the scientific study of logic. His philosophical treatises on metaphysics, ethics, politics, and aesthetics remain more than two thousand years later among the most profound works ever written on these subjects. His scientific work produced groundbreaking achievements in biology, psychology, zoology, meteorology, and astronomy. His later influence was so magnetic that during the Middle Ages he was referred to simply as "the Philosopher."

Aristotle did not agree with Plato's theory of ideas. He contended that universal essences have no subsistence—i.e., existence in themselves—apart from that which they have within the particulars. For example, humanity or justice, and so on, do not exist independently in some vague metaphysical world of ideas but only as an elements in specific individual substances. Thus, whereas Plato viewed knowledge as a remembering of those ideas that already were possessed in the soul, Aristotle was of the mind that the acquisition of understanding and knowledge involved an abstraction of the common essential elements shared by individual entities. Sense experience was the beginning of knowledge, according to Aristotle.

Aristotle stressed the importance of final causes in understanding reality. According to his viewpoint, nature is teleological—and all natural processes have a purpose.

Aristotle's writings are lectures that were given to the students attending his Lyceum. From them, there evolved a *Corpus Aristotelicum,* which is the body of the works of Aristotle. They included works on logic, natural sciences, metaphysics, ethics and politics, and poetics.

Logic

His works on logic (*Organon* = tool) are some of the most significant works ever on this subject. He was the first to examine and analyze the content of thought and the form that should be used in argumentation. This was the beginning of formal logic. It became by way of thinkers such as Boethius and Petrus Hispanus the foundation of traditional logic.

Aristotle begins his treatises with the simple idea or concept that we possess about reality or anything whatsoever. A concept is an abstraction. Concepts are mental abstractions, mental signs, and symbols that refer to classes of concrete things or realities. These concepts are abstract from the existence of the thing referred to. They refer to a thing according to its common essential characteristics. There are many epistemological and metaphysical knotty points that stem from this simple explanation. I shall treat of this below in a later analysis. At any rate, according to Aristotle, one simple idea or concept in itself expresses what is called a *category.*

> Simple expressions (ideas, concepts) express substance—man, the horse (quantity)—two inches long (quality)—white, grammatical (relation)—greater, place—in the market place (time).

However, both in his discourses on logic and in his philosophical treatises, especially when he treats of metaphysics, Aristotle holds that the very first principles cannot be proven. That means that, according to him, there are some proposition, sentences, or principles that are "just true" in themselves. Deductive arguments can thus follow from these self-evident principles. There is no other prior proof that can be given. As Aristotle states,

> Things are "true" and "primary" which are believed on the strength not of anything else but of themselves: for in regard to the first principles of science (knowledge) it is improper to ask any further for the why and wherefore of them. (*Topics*)

The counterpart in Aristotle's thought is the *inductive* method or induction. Induction is going from the particular truth or truths to a general truth. There is some difficulty with this method as it relies upon knowledge of too many particulars in order to come to any certain new truth. Therefore, it seems to lead only to probability. Nevertheless it is this method that is used in science.

In modern times, there is some difficulty in explaining the nature of deductive and inductive arguments. Nevertheless, Aristotle began the examination of these two types of arguments. They are still used today, though with some adaptations.

Following in the footsteps of Socrates and Plato, Aristotle emphasized that the *definition* played a prominent role in logic. Unless there are commonly accepted definitions, it is impossible to carry on fruitful arguments. Commonly accepted definitions are often hard to express. They must contain those characteristics that are essential to the subject in question. Moreover, they must clearly manifest how one object of a given class distinguishes itself from objects in another class. What, for example, is a commonly accepted definition of what a human being is? What is a terrorist? What is democracy? Many modern ethical concerns revolve around the acceptance of or the rejection of fundamental definitions.

Although studies in logic have advanced tremendously in modern times, the insights of Aristotle, if no longer fully considered valid or complete in their entirety, still constitute a core element in the sphere of formal logic.

Metaphysics

As mentioned, Aristotle had written a number of treatises that dealt with the natural sciences. He wrote other treatises that dealt with realities that he considered the bedrock or substratum of all entities. These treatises were placed in the compiled works *after* the tracts on natural science (i.e., physics). In Greek, it was expressed *meta ta physika.* Hence, the word *metaphysics* was used as the title of one of Aristotle's books, and its subsequent use as a branch of philosophy was an historical fluke or accident.

Aristotle, although one of the most brilliant pupils of Plato, parted ways with Plato's theory of ideas (or theory of forms). He was aware of the difficulties in trying to maintain Plato's theory. One such difficulty was that if the existing "Ideas" in the world of ideas were constant, eternal, and unchanging, how could they ever *be or become* the structure of concrete things that were persistently shifting and changing?

Secondly, how could the impermanent realities of the "real" world share in the eternal and permanent realities of the "Idea world" of Plato? How could they be a *cause* of sensible things? How could static and unchangeable ideas be a principle of *activity* so as to affect sensible realities?

In his later works, Plato did suggest that the world of ideas was in reality the "Intelligence of the Divine Being." He also suggested that the "Good" or absolute Goodness was both *static* and *dynamic.* It was thus the force that caused and is causing the existence of all sensible things or realities. Although Aristotle did not accept or develop these solutions, they were developed centuries later by some followers of Plato and by some Christian philosophers.

Plato also suggested a theory that there was something midway between the eternal ideas and the sensible world. This "something" was the geometrical and/or mathematical realities that were the underlying substance of sensible entities. (Strangely enough, in our times, a theory somewhat like that of Plato is once again becoming popular with some philosopher/scientists as they research the world of atomic particles and its effects upon a "truer" vision of what "matter" and the world of "change" might be.)

Aristotle thought that the arguments that he used to reject the existence of a world of Ideas also held when he questioned the validity of Plato's theories that geometry or mathematics is the basis or substratum of the concrete thing.

> Again, it would seem impossible that the substance and that of which it is the substance should exist apart; how, therefore, could the Ideas, being the substances of things, exist apart?
>
> Again, if the Forms are numbers, how can they be causes? Is it because existing things are other number, e.g. one number is man, another is Socrates, another Callias? Why then are the one set of numbers causes of the other set?
> (*Metaphysics*)

Aristotle's conclusion was that the essence of things exists in the things themselves and not in some cloudy metaphysical world of Ideas (or world of Forms, as expressed differently).

Aristotle, however, did not dismiss out of hand the notion that finite reality was essentially dualistic. That is, two essential elements made up finite existing things. His dualism, however, was not the dualism of Plato—namely, on the hand the sphere of eternal Ideas and on the other hand sensible realities. *He was convinced that ideas or essences were concretized in particular things.*

Aristotle theorized that all changeable reality was a mixture of matter and form. His theory is called *hylomorphism* (Greek: *hyle* = matter, *morphe* = form). Both matter and form exist simultaneously. In finite entities, pure matter and pure form cannot exist alone and independently. I will consider later Aristotle's notion that the "unmoved mover" is pure form and is not finite. Secondly, there are various interpretations concerning Aristotle's opinion as to whether the human soul, which is the "form" of human beings, can exist independently. *The soul is considered the "entelechy" of the body. Entelechy is a notion in the theories of Aristotle whereby he explained that all organic entities have a purpose for which they are striving within their essential makeup.* The soul is not material. At the same time, the soul is not separable from the body.

The soul does not exist without a body and yet is not itself a kind of body. For it is not a body, but something which belongs to a body, and for this reason exists in a body, and in a body of such-and-such a kind. (*On the Soul*)

Matter is the measurable, the quantifiable element of the thing. *Form* is that which makes the thing what it is . . . its "kindness," so to speak, in answer to the question: *What kind of thing is this?* Form thoroughly coalesces with matter in the concrete and individual entity.

Aristotle molded a synthesis that he thought could explain the world of "Becoming" or of the apparently continuously changing. Matter was the substratum, the empty, amorphous, indefinite, and obscure clump of *dynamic possibility or potentiality* (Greek: *dynamis*, Latin: *potentia*). It is the essence of potentiality. Matter is energized and given *a full actual reality* (Greek: *energeia*) by the form. The form exists not in some metaphysical world of ideas, according to Aristotle, but in the individual thing itself. Forms appeared and disappeared as physical things changed.

Aristotle conceived of a purposeful unfolding or evolvement of entities. A goal or purpose was always embedded in this change from the potential to the actual. The purpose of things was to play a central part in his metaphysics.

On an *abstract* level, Aristotle's matter/form theory can be expressed as a potency/act theory. *Potency* is the *ability* within a thing to act or to become something else (i.e., be *transformed*), to actualize some power it has, or to be acted upon. *Act* means what the entity actually *is* right now. Or it can mean, if we narrow the concept down to specific movements within the individual thing, what the individual is *doing* at the moment.

For example, humans have the potency (i.e., power, capability) to think, but they are not always actually thinking. For Aristotle, the capability to think and the actualization of this power to think (i.e., thinking) were distinct elements of the total process of thinking or intellectualizing. Thinking is a mixture of potency and act. The potency/act theory becomes important and essential for understanding much of Aristotle's philosophy. The little seedling that is buried in the ground has the potency to become a full-grown oak tree. The oak tree is its actualization. But one already knows that the seed contains within itself the potency to be thus actualized. Its entelechy strives to be fulfilled or actualized in this way.

The Four Causes

Aristotle cited four basic reasons that determine the makeup of entities. *He thought that everything—every reality—could be understood better by examining and coming to an understanding of its "causes."* A cause is something that is in some way *responsible* for and *influences* the thing that one is investigating.

Aristotle came to these conclusions concerning causality from his study and interpretation of the thought of earlier pre-Socratic thinkers. The four causes that Aristotle enumerates are the following:

1. The *material* cause: the matter that something is made of.
    (This answers the question: "What is the thing made of?")
2. The *formal* cause: that which makes the thing the "kind" of thing it is.
    ("Why is it this kind of thing?")
    This formal cause can be:
    a) artificial: e.g. a desk. It has a certain "shape" that makes it a desk"
    b) natural: e.g. it belongs to a "species" of a thing—a dog, a cat, a man.
3. The *efficient* cause: that which moves of makes something.
    (This answers the question: "Who or what moved it or made it?") E.g. The mover of a chair. The parents generate a child.

Aristotle applied this notion of efficient cause to theorize about the *first efficient cause or the first mover* of all that exists. He argued that there must be one efficient cause that is *not* caused by any other efficient cause. Otherwise, he argued, nothing could either come into existence or exist in the present. That is, nothing can come from nothing, but something cannot come from nothing. He called this being the "unmoved mover." The "unmoved mover" is pure act and contains no potentiality. It is the uncaused *caused*. There has been controversy concerning the scientific validity of this theory of Aristotle argument over centuries.

4. The *final* cause: the reason "why" something is.
(This answers the question "Why or to what purpose does this thing exist?")

Cause and Effect are metaphysical principles for Aristotle. That is, all Being (except for the unmoved mover) shares in some kind of causality.

Aristotle analyzes things according to the categories that are mentioned. He breaks down categories into two fundamental categories. The first is substance, and the second is the category of accidents. Aristotle used the term *symbebekota*, which in Latin was "*accidentia*." Hence, we have the term *accident* in English.

A *substance* means something that exists by itself (a man, a horse, a flower, etc.).

An *accident,* on the other hand, means something that exists only in or through another thing. It cannot exist in and of itself (white, dark, tall, long). It means that which a substance can do without and still remain the same substance.

Applying the notions of potency and act, the four causes, and the categories, Aristotle developed his theories on the nature of reality. He thought that the primary and first subject of analysis was "Being Itself." For everything was a being and hence shared in "Being." Metaphysics for Aristotle was an investigation of Being Itself. The notion of metaphysics stemming from treatises written by Aristotle having been placed *after* the books on physics, took on the meaning of realities *above* and *beyond* the sensible and physical world. The realities existed and could be investigated. Metaphysics became a facet of philosophy.

The pre-Socratics, whom we have written about above, were searching for the one common element from which all other things sprang. Or they were searching for the one common element that infused itself into all things. Plato found these elements in his world of Ideas. He found the one *single* element in the Idea of "the Good." The Good penetrated all of reality. The Good shrouded and swathed all other Ideas. For they were *all* "good."

Aristotle came to a different standpoint. The one fundamental, all-encompassing, and intangible substratum of all of reality is *"Being."* That is, everything is a being or shares in Being. Therefore, for Aristotle, the first subject of metaphysics is "Being." Aristotle considered the study of "Being" to be different from the study of being(s), which is the subject of other sciences. The particular natural science cuts off, so to speak, a portion of Being and views this dissected portion of Being as its proper subject. Metaphysics, or the study of "Being" as such, studies the cause of the *whole of reality.* The subject of Being is immaterial and bodiless. It treats of abstractions. It treats of the Ideas that are found in Plato's world of Ideas, but according to Aristotle, the search is begun and completed along a different route.

Aristotle was an empiricist. That is, he began the search for knowledge with experiences of the concrete individual things that were before him. His examination of reality started with the empirical facts.

This led him to note the similarities and dissimilarities of the objects that he was studying. In botany and zoology, for example, this led him to classify the different species of plants and animals that he was studying. His empirical investigations led him to abstractions. He classified objects according to their general similarities, which became the genus, and their specific similarities, which became the species. These concepts were abstractions. Finally there was the individual object with its unique individual differences.

Aristotle began with the individual concrete object and developed his theories by beginning with individual differences, then going up the ladder to specific differences, to generic differences until he reached the one super-genus that is shared by everything—that is, "Being" or more concretely put, "Thingness."

The investigation of "Being" is a real science according to Aristotle. It is a science that leads to wisdom. He did not lose this conviction that the purpose of philosophy was to make the student of philosophy "wise."

> There is a science which investigates being as being and the
> attributes which belong to this in virtue of its own nature. Now

this is not the same as any of the so-called special sciences; for none of these others treats universally of being as being. They cut off a part of being and investigate the attributes of this part; this is what the mathematical sciences for instance do. Now since we are seeking the first principles and the highest causes, clearly there must be some thing to which these belong in virtue of its own nature. If then those who sought the elements of existing things were seeking these same principles, it is necessary that the elements must be elements of being not by accident but just because it is being. Therefore it is of being as being that we also must grasp the first cause. (*Metaphysics*)

Man—Knowledge

Like Plato, Aristotle was also of the opinion that the human being is a mixture of soul and body. The soul is that which makes a human being a human being. It is the "form" of the body. *It is spiritual and not material.* Aristotle demonstrates the truth that the soul is spiritual in an inductive manner. He reasons that *man knows the essences of things.* The knowledge of essences is a *process* involving a *power that is nonmaterial.*

So the subject (i.e., the soul) of this power or faculty (i.e., the intellect) must also be spiritual. The human soul is the reason (formal) why a man is a man.

In general then, according to Aristotle, a soul is a *substance* or actualization of natural bodies that *have life in potentiality.* The *human* soul is the actualization of a *human body.*

The human soul, according to Aristotle, has three branches, functions, or parts (later interpreters of Aristotle were to discuss whether man has three souls or one soul with three functions!), each of which fulfills a separate function. The lowest is the nutritive soul. It is akin to the plant soul of that form of life, which is found among the plants in our surrounding nature. Its function and purpose is to support and sustain the nutritive and growth processes in the body.

A second branch of the soul is the sensitive branch. This branch of the soul supports and sustains the animal part of human nature. It is the cause of self-movement, sensation, and emotions in man.

The highest branch of the soul is **the** *mind (intellect)*. The mind as a spiritual power is the seat of thinking, reasoning, knowing, willing, and other intellectual activities.

It is in view of the above theories that Aristotle defines a *human being* as a *rational animal*. The human being belongs both to the animal world and to the semidivine world of intellect and reason. Whether Aristotle thought the soul was immortal or not is an open question.

The mind possesses a singular and special status of pre-eminence in human beings. Aristotle separates the higher part of the soul or the mind into different spheres. Each sphere is a unique power or potentiality.

The highest form of knowledge—*cognition or intellection*—takes place in the highest part of the soul. Aristotle approaches epistemology, or the meaning of knowledge, in an empirical fashion. *All knowledge begins with sense experience.* It *begins* with the concrete, particular, changeable phenomenon. Cognition does *not occur*, however, in any degree of sense experience. Cognition is not only the accumulation of and association of sense impressions in the physical brain.

The highest form of knowledge for Aristotle is intellectual knowledge. *The intellect is therefore a potency or a power of the higher part of the soul to "actualize" in the intellect the essence of the thing that is known.* Intellectual knowledge is essentially in its beginning stages *dependent* upon *sense knowledge* and sense perception. The highest form of knowledge, intellectual knowledge, *goes beyond this sense perception.* The object of intellectual knowledge is the abstract, the universal, and the immutable essence of the object.

Universal means an idea that is applied to many things within a class of things in the same way. The abstract means the concept or idea in the intellect that cuts away the element of existence from the object and views *intellectually only the essential, unchanging elements of the thing known.* It means taking an "intellectual X-ray" picture of the object. The inner elements of the essence of the object are thus revealed. This intellectual abstraction is called a knowledge of the "intelligible." *Intelligible means that which is knowable in the concrete individual thing is able to be intellectually grasped. Intelligible means the ability of the defining properties or elements of an object to be intellectually recognized and understood.*

Knowledge in a fully human sense does not stop with these initial *apprehensions* **or** *perceptions*. The higher form of the soul has the power to *reason* **or** *think*. It can understand the association between many apprehensions or concepts. It can make judgments. The mind can develop both inductive and deductive arguments to deepen the significance and meaning of that which is apprehended. It can reflect upon a single apprehension and analyze it more deeply. The intellect using reason can seek to *comprehend* the object it is intellectually viewing. To comprehend means to know all there is to know about an object.

In summary, the human mind is empowered with a power of abstraction and generalization by which it removes the veil of individualizing characteristics and brings out and leaves revealed the actually intelligible. It is these elements in entities or things that are the object of intellectual knowledge according to Aristotle.

In this theory, intellectual knowledge is developed from sense knowledge. Aristotle thus makes a distinction between a "passive" intellect and an "active" intellect. That is the process of knowledge involves a "phantasm" or material "picture" of the object existing *outside* the mind being formed *in* the mind. The intellect then, by the *active intellect, conceptually spiritualizes* this *passive impression* and draws out the essence of the known object. *Intellectually the knower thus becomes the thing known* (mentally, not physically!). *Aristotle did not clearly explain how this is possible.* Given the hypothetical existence of two polarities within human nature—that is the soul, which is immaterial, and the body, which is material—how can the two interact? Aristotle did not comment.

In later centuries, many philosophers, especially some medieval Arab philosophers, deduced the notion of a "world soul" from Aristotle's teachings concerning the "active" intellect. The problem is bound up with the perennial problem surrounding the "spirit/body" features within the nature of a human being and how these two polarities can ever interact. That is, how can matter act upon spirit (i.e., nonmaterial) or how can spirit act upon matter.

Aristotle was of the opinion that the act of thinking is the divine element in human nature. Man is like unto the divine when man is actually thinking.

Thinking in itself deals with that which is best in itself, and which is thinking in the fullest sense with that which is best in the fullest sense. And thought thinks on itself because it shares in the nature of the object of thought; for it becomes an object of thought in coming into contact with and thinking its objects, so that thought and object of thought are the same. For that which is capable of receiving the object of thought, i.e. the essence, is thought. But it is active when it possesses this object. Therefore the possession rather that the receptivity is the divine element which thought seems to contain, and the act of contemplation is what is most pleasant and best. If, then, God is always in that good state in which we sometimes are, this compels our wonder; and if in a better this compels it yet more. And God is in a better state. And life also belongs to God; for the actuality of thought is life, and God is that actuality; and God's self-dependent actuality is life most good and eternal. (*Metaphysics*)

Ethics

As to Aristotle's views on the purpose of human life, these are to be found in his *Nicomachean Ethics*. This work (named after Aristotle's son Nicomachus) is universally considered one of the great books of moral philosophy. *It ranges from detailed analyses of such concepts as choosing, deliberating, and wishing, to a vision of man's highest happiness as a life devoted to the exercise of contemplation and pure reason.*

The book possesses some organizational difficulties, since, like his other treatises, it consists of texts of his lectures as preserved in his students' notes. However, unity is provided by central themes, among which are the commitment to viewing the good as the fulfillment of human nature, the emphasis upon a close relationship between ethics and the interests of society, and the need to distinguish moral from intellectual virtue.

According to Aristotle, *moral* virtues, which we might call "goodness of character," are formed by habit. *One becomes good by doing what is good over and over until it becomes a good habit that is easily done.* Repeated acts of justice and self-control result in a just, self-controlled person, who not only performs just and self-controlled actions but does so from a fixed moral character. *Intellectual* virtues, on the other hand, which we might refer to as "intelligence," are acquired through teaching, and they require foresight and sophisticated intelligence. Both the moral virtues and the intellectual virtues or dispositions of character must be practiced in order for one to *become* and *remain* a truly virtuous person.

Both sorts of virtues, the intellectual and the moral, ensure that man chooses the right means to achieve a good end or result of his actions. *The final goal or end of man, for Aristotle, is happiness.* He is the first to admit that it is difficult to say concretely what this happiness is. But it did seem reasonable to him to state that no matter what action a man performs, he does it ultimately to be happy. This is true even when one willingly undergoes something extremely painful, such as a painful operation. The ultimate goal is eventually to become well and to be able to live happily.

In opposition to the Socratic viewpoint—namely that a person who knows the good will necessarily do the good—Aristotle insists upon acknowledging the phenomenon of *moral weakness:* the situation, so easy to recognize and yet so difficult to explain, in which *individuals can act contrary* to what they believe to be for the best. Typically, he emphasizes that a theory that denies the existence of moral weakness is at variance with observed facts.

Aristotle used the above ideas in his discussion on ethics and morality. He considered that an understanding of both the nature of man and his ultimate purpose (teleological approach) as essential to answering questions concerning the perfection or imperfection of human actions.

What is the final (ultimate) goal, end, or purpose to human existence? In asking the question, two words are emphasized: *human* and *purpose.* Both must be analyzed before attempting to answer the question.

Aristotle then examined what the nature of the human being is—i.e., he is a rational animal with all that that implies. Therefore, the purpose of human existence must in some way be drawn from this definition. Aristotle thought that the uniqueness of man is that he possesses a spiritual soul with intellectual powers. *The intellectual powers are the intellect and the will* (the power to intellectualize and the power to freely choose what one desires to do). These powers are the highest faculties that man possesses.

Aristotle thought that human beings wish to become "perfected." That is, they wish to use their talents (powers) to the best of their abilities. To put it another way, their *happiness* is the attainment of what is really *good* for them. Aristotle thought that happiness was the ultimate desire of all human beings. The *intermediate ways* of gaining this happiness differed with the individual; each one's idea of what would make him happy and each one's talents differed, but the ultimate *purpose in general* was the same: to become happy.

Therefore, like Socrates, Aristotle thought that it is necessary to "know yourself" if one is to obtain happiness. *To achieve happiness, one has to know what one is in a human sense and also in an individual sense.* Happiness will only come about by doing what is good—according to our nature and according to our individual talents. Aristotle claimed that this kind of ethical knowledge could *never* be mathematically certain knowledge. *We can only reach an approximation and do our best.* Ethics is thus a *practical* study. It has to do with the concrete man and the concrete situations that accompany life.

The perfecting of a human being comes about by trying to live a "virtuous" life. To live a life in accordance with good habits will make it easy to do good. A good habit (virtue) is brought about by doing good acts over and over until it becomes easy to do them and one feels good about it. A bad habit (a vice) means that one does evil actions over and over until it becomes easy to act in such a way.

Good habits (virtues) affect the intellect, the will, and the body. They affect the whole person. Aristotle was following Socrates when he taught that one must know the good before one could will to do it. Nevertheless, Aristotle claimed the will is basically free to make a choice between good and evil. To know what is good for one to do does *not necessarily cause* one to do the good action. In this respect, Aristotle differed from Socrates and Plato.

Aristotle recognized that fear, ignorance, society pressure, etc. do influence free will. Sometimes, such pressures can even destroy the possibility of a free choice. Still, he emphasized the natural power to choose freely within human beings. The really virtuous man is one who knows what is really good to do and then freely chooses to do the good action.

Aristotle systematized a method to know the value of moral actions. These actions could be viewed with a relation to one's own person or in relation to others in society. Knowledge of a virtue assists one to act according to the virtue and thus be a virtuous person.

He discussed the nature of a truly free human act. He thought it was one that was carried out with *sufficient deliberative knowledge* beforehand. Insufficient knowledge leads to error. Insufficient knowledge can be culpable if it is a knowledge that one should have had before acting. Actions proceeding from culpable ignorance are acts of *negligence.*

He thought that many virtues are midway between two extreme vices. For example, courage is between the two vices of foolhardiness and cowardice.

Society and Politics

Aristotle's metaphysical and ethical theories penetrated his teaching about man and society. There should be a harmony between the good of the individual and the good of the state. He stated that man is a *social animal* by nature. He therefore thought differently about the origins of the state than Plato and others did. The origin was not due to man's weaknesses, which lean toward greed and hatred and thus necessitate, out of sheer utilitarian motives, an agreement whereby men could live peacefully together. On the contrary, according to Aristotle, the origin was due to a *positive characteristic* embedded in the essence of man. Man is really a political animal and tends to group himself around and with other human beings. There is therefore a common happiness to be achieved (as evidenced in the human constitution).

What is good for the individual should then be in some way good for the state. What is good for the state should be good for the individual. The purpose of the state is that a good common life leads to happiness for the individuals within the state. However, everyone should be treated according to his or her abilities. Systems of government, laws, and customs are developed along these ideas.

Aristotle began his comments on politics by examining 150 extant constitutions. He then went on to express his ideas on government. He felt that monarchies, aristocracies, and semidemocracies were good forms of government. On the other hand tyrannies, oligarchies, and pure democracies were inferior forms of government. He did not give any special preference to any of the three good forms of government. He stressed that the family and private property were important to the state. Slavery was considered natural.

CHAPTER SIX

Later Greek and Roman Philosophy

Various schools of philosophy took their direction from Socrates, Plato, and Aristotle. The Academy of Plato endured until AD 529. It was then officially closed by Emperor Justinian. Platonism, or philosophies that followed essentially the themes of Plato, has never died out completely. Early Christianity used Plato's philosophy to explain its beliefs. Thus a so-called Christian philosophy developed. Platonism was a prominent philosophy during the Renaissance in Europe. Some Platonic thought is enjoying a resurgence in modern times due to research going on in theoretical atomic physics.

The philosophy of Aristotle became the predominant philosophy during the European Middle Ages. It was used to explain Christian beliefs. During this period, Platonism faded into the background somewhat. The philosophy of Aristotle, due to its empiricism perhaps, became a favorite philosophy of the English-speaking world. It is still an important area of philosophy in many universities. The philosophy has been modified to harmonize with the findings of modern science.

In the nineteenth century, a German historian, Droysen, coined the term "Hellenism." Hellenism stood for the spread and permeation of Greek culture throughout the Middle East. This process was caused by the expeditions of conquest by Alexander the Great. Alexander the Great had conquered the powerful Persian Empire and then took his armies all the way to India. He conquered Egypt and other surrounding territories.

Although his united empire was short lived—it broke apart soon after his death in 323 BC—the language and culture of Greece endured. However, this culture was influenced by the various oriental cultures. Greek culture thus became more cosmopolitan and no longer bound down to the city-state type environment and outlook of previous centuries. The Greek language slowly became the official court language throughout the Middle East. The age of Hellenism lasted from the death of Alexander the Great until about 1 BC.

After the death of Aristotle in 322 BC, philosophers turned more inward and concentrated on the ethical life. Many were interested in philosophy as the culmination of a search for inner freedom and peace of mind. Four major schools of philosophy endured in Athens. Plato's Academy thrived. After the death of Aristotle, one of his students, Theophrastus, founded the Peripatetic School in 317 BC, which continued in the traditions of Aristotle. Epicurus started to teach around 307 BC; Zeno of Citium, the Stoic, came to Athens and was teaching in the Stoa by 302 BC. These schools of philosophy exhibited, commented on, transformed, and taught the four major currents of philosophy— *Stoic, Epicurean, Academic (Plato),* **and** *Peripatetic (Aristotle).*

Epicurus

Epicurus is a significant philosopher of the Hellenistic period. He was a materialist and an empiricist. He lived from around 341-271 BC. He settled in Athens around 306 BC and founded a garden/school. This was a mixture of a philosophical school and a communal lifestyle for the residents of the garden/school. Along with Stoicism, Epicureanism became a major current of philosophy until the arrival of Christian philosophy. Almost none of the writings of Epicurus are extant. We learn of his thoughts through other sources. The Roman poet Lucretius (94-55 BC) and the Roman writer and politician Cicero (106-43 BC) wrote on Epicureanism.

Epicurus was convinced that a human being could obtain knowledge of the world by relying on the senses in a rational way. He rejected the opinion that a human being has an immaterial soul.

The goal of human existence was tranquility or peace of mind. This could be obtained by limiting one's desires and keeping them under control. One had also to lose all fear of death and of the gods.

Epicurus was a not a hedonist in the narrow sense of the term. He did not hold that physical pleasure alone was the goal of human existence.

He began his ethical considerations by agreeing with Aristotle that the highest good is that which is valued and desired for its own sake, and not for the sake of anything else. He also agrees with Aristotle that this goal is happiness. *Epicurus identifies happiness with pleasure.*

Epicurus takes an empirical approach to substantiate his claim. He sees that people *do value pleasure* for its own sake, regardless of the theoretical notions of philosophers. There is an element of *utilitarianism* in his philosophy. We human beings do those things that are *useful* to bring about pleasure.

The *highest form of pleasure* for Epicurus is a *mental pleasure.* He thought that if desires were satisfied, one would achieve a condition of tranquility and peace (*ataraxia*). Therefore, since it is impossible to fulfill all desires, those desires should be controlled that draw one away from tranquility, and those desires should be fulfilled that are useful to achieve a state of tranquility. Hence, a virtuous and ascetic life is recommended and useful for obtaining ultimate pleasure.

In summary, Epicurus thought that feelings of pleasure and pain constitute the fundamental criteria for what is to be considered desirable and valuable and what is to be avoided as harmful.

The Skeptics

Skepticism had always been a trend of philosophical thought in philosophy. It has animated the thought of philosophers like David Hume and those of today. **In its radical form, skepticism means fundamentally doubting the possibility to know the truth about anything whatsoever.** A logical inconsistency with holding such a principle is that the principle itself is thrown into doubt. Thus there is never a starting point to philosophize.

In its milder form, skepticism means to doubt this or that proposition or belief. In this form, skepticism is a tool of all philosophers.

Originally, skepticism was a method to achieve peace of mind (*ataraxia*). Skepticism began with the thoughts of Pyrrho of Elis (365-275 BC). His thoughts were systematically represented by Sextus Empiricus (around AD 200-250). *Skepticism was seen at that time as an art of thinking whereby one could withdraw or suspend any judgment concerning propositions that claim to state the truth. Skeptics were convinced that mental turmoil and confusion stem from an inner urge to know things and value them. Suspending judgment was supposed to still and quiet this powerful inner desire and thus lead to a sort of attitudinal indifference, which in turn would generate peace of mind.*

An inner desire to know was viewed as the beginning of philosophizing by Aristotle and others like him over the centuries. For the skeptics, this desire was viewed as a purposeless desire and could lead nowhere. Hence the way to philosophize was to become convinced of this fact. Philosophizing according to the Skeptics was, in a sense, a negative experience. A negation of the activity aroused by this purposeless desire to know could be engendered by simply withholding judgment.

The essential traits of the ancient schools of skepticism are some of the following. Because of these observable traits, the skeptics came to the conclusion that knowledge of the truth was impossible to come by.

1. There are so many differing kinds of living things.
2. Human beings are so different all over the world.
3. Sense organs are differently disposed.
4. The subjective situations of human beings are so different. (The vision of truth depends on moods, psychological conditions, points of view, language, and so on.)
5. Differences exist relating to the position of an object, its distance from the person who wants to know, and the surroundings of the object.
6. There are relative differences between appearances and actual perceptions.
7. The frequency or lack of frequency of impressions received in a human being from objects presumed to exist outside the mind make true knowledge impossible.
8. The differences in education, customs, religious beliefs, and philosophical convictions that influence the human population cause knowledge to be relative.

The early skeptics realized that in moral situations, one must act and one cannot withhold judgments indefinitely or nothing would be done. They recognized the validity of everyday common-sense-directed experiences and judgments for the here-and-now ethical decisions of everyday life. A skeptic could only make ethical judgments in a nondogmatic manner relative to the absolute truth value of the actions.

A Socratic-skeptical doctrine crept into the New Academy, the philosophical descendent of Plato's original Academy. Two famous names were Arcesilaus (315-20 BC) and Carneades (213-128 BC). They claimed that criteria for absolute truth did not exist. One could only expect to know *probabilities concerning the truth.* This phase of skepticism in the Academy seems not to have influenced for very long the later development of Neo-Platonism.

Stoicism

Changes in emphasis in philosophy were effected at this later time by a new power that was emerging in Italy in the West. That force was the power and might of **Rome.** Rome began as a small city near the center of Italy. Over centuries, it spread its tentacles over all of Italy. In time, North Africa, Spain, lands that now encompass Belgium, France, and parts of Germany, parts of England, Egypt, and most of the former empire of Alexander Great made up the ever-expanding Roman Empire.

Although Greece succumbed militarily and politically to Rome, Rome maintained a fascination with Greek culture. Greeks went to Rome to build Roman temples and buildings, Greek sculpture and art was Romanized, and Greek became the second language of the Roman Empire. The first language was Latin. Greek philosophy did not suffer. One famous Roman poet, Horace, expressed pithily in Latin, *"Graecia victa Romanum victorem vicit."* Translated, this sentence means, "Greece, after it had been conquered, vanquished the Roman victors."

The Romans, however, were a practical people. They had not much use for metaphysics in too great detail. They were interested in ethics, natural law, and science, in so far as science would assist them in construction and warfare. Roman philosophy took on a practical bent. The Romans who were interested in philosophy were searching for a philosophy that would offer peace of mind. They desired philosophical convictions by which they could live with some amount of equilibrium in a huge imperialistic world burdened with discord, guile, deceit, wars, and uncertainty. They also were inclined toward a philosophy that would blend the ethical dimensions and actions of the individual with the needs of the Roman state and Roman law.

One philosophical stream was to become synonymous with Roman culture. This philosophy was *Stoicism.* Stoicism had a long history. It was a philosophy that began in Hellenistic times in Greece around 336 BC. It lasted into late antiquity. Zeno of Citium, Cleanthes, and Chrysippus were early Greek philosophers who gave substance to early Stoicism. Posidonius and others imported the tenets of Stoicism to Rome around 135 BC. Lucius Annaeus Seneca was a celebrated Roman Stoic. The Roman Emperor Marcus Aurelius (121-180 AD) was another famous Roman Stoic. The freed slave Epictetus (around AD 50-130) was also a renowned teacher of Stoicism.

According to Stoicism, all things, even God, were material. Stoicism considered fire as the one single material element that pulsated in all things. Other elements—air, water, earth, and other things—were produced by and impregnated with fire. Fire is also the divine "soul" that permeates all things and moves them according to reason. The Stoics thought of the universe as a great cycle of movement. It began with fire and will end in a massive conflagration. Early Christianity took over this conviction and believed also that the earth, time, and space would pass away in a fiery dissolution accompanied by falling stars and an all-encompassing fire.

God, for the Stoics, is the primal creative force. He is the first cause of all things. As "Reason" (Logos), he is in all things. The entire cosmos is seen as a living thing, the soul of which is divine. The divine soul is material. The early Greek Stoics thought of God as the most ethereal form of matter. God was the all-pervasive reason abiding in everything. The Cosmos was God. The universe is therefore pantheistic.

Hence, a reasonable plan and an eternal law direct the universe. There is thus a purpose, harmony, and divine design within the cosmos. Everything is in order. This established *order* is called fate (*L. fatum*). The established *goal* is called providence (*L. providentia*).

These metaphysical and theological convictions concerning Reason, Fate, and Providence provided a foundation for *Stoic ethics.* A basic principle or guideline was that no human being had continuous and absolute control over external goods and present or impending occurrences in life. The inner *attitude* that one possesses toward these external goods and events was the only thing that a person had control over. Philosophy was a means to recognize, understand, and *accept* nature and all of the natural processes that occur. Once one accepts nature for what it truly is, one can then work *with* nature, rather than *against* nature.

The ethical goal was to achieve happiness—a theme similar to that of Aristotle. *Concretely stated, Stoic happiness was peace of mind or peace of soul. A person should strive to get rid of any emotional or mental disturbance that disturbs the soul.* The mental freedom that was thereby achieved was called *Apathy*. By Roman times, this did *not* mean *complete* disinterestedness or resignation, although this was the thought of some early Greek Stoics. Roman Stoicism was inclined to the view that a person should strive to be *reasonably unaffected* by things and events. Reasonably unaffected meant one conforms one's inner attitude to be in line with nature itself as it is pervaded by providence. In Roman Stoicism, Providence was seen at times as a kind of spiritual divinity or quality of the spiritually divine. The *ultimate goal* of nature was also an *essential element* of nature. It was not separate and "out there." Freedom from the scourge of inordinate affections was thus understood as living according to Providence. *The wise person in Stoicism harmonizes his (her) individual nature with Nature itself. The wise person understands that virtue is the only good that is worth possessing.* Vice is evil. External things are trivial in themselves. One should seek to be unconcerned about them.

As with other Greek philosophers, morality was viewed as a virtuous life lived according to the bidding of reason. A life of virtue requires knowledge of the meaning and power of nature and the laws of nature.

The early Greek Stoics lived by severe dictates of reason. They attempted to eradicate fully and completely all emotions. They tended to live a life of poverty, unconcern, and complete disdain for the affairs of the world. The Roman Stoic smoothed over and softened the harshness embodied in these earlier Stoic teachings. The Roman Stoics acknowledged the innate weaknesses in human beings and were more sensitive to them than the older Greek Stoics were. Apathy in the fullest sense was not a part of Roman Stoicism. They regarded reasonable emotions as necessary and valuable ingredients of human existence. **Nevertheless,** *irrational emotions* were to be avoided and uprooted. Logical and purposeful thought and contemplation about the reasons for the presence of these unwanted emotions were methods that were much used in order to root out such emotions.

According to the ancient Greek Stoics, all external things were seen as trivial. By Roman times, this view had become milder. The Roman Stoics thought that some things were less trivial than others. When all was said and done, there were still things over which one had no control. Still, a limited freedom within a universe governed by the force of predetermination was recognized and fostered. This freedom was the freedom of the inner faculty of judgment (the will) within human beings. Though man was powerless over most things—external affairs and the acts of other human beings—man was not powerless over what kind of attitude one could take against these things. One could make a decision to hold an attitude of indifference. One could also develop an inner attitude of indifference toward the evils one could not avoid—suffering, sickness, persecution, the opinions of others, and death.

Another central theme of Stoicism was the conviction that an ethical and virtuous life must also be oriented to the community, the state, and later the empire. Ancient Stoicism was individualistic. One should concentrate only on the self. It seemed selfish. By Roman times, this attitude had been moderated. Under Roman Stoicism, *all men were considered to be brothers, each of whom was allotted a due place of worth in nature.* A conclusion following this conviction was that everyone had a share in the life of the state. All in the empire had duties and obligations to the Roman government. An ethical and virtuous life must also be oriented to the community.

This was a conviction embraced in later Christian Stoicism. The Christians naturally possessed different reasons for this conviction. They believed that, as an ideal, all human beings were, and are, worthy of respect because all are creatures and children of God. Unfortunately, such a principle has never been fully adhered to by all. A principle similar to this tenet of Stoicism has become an underlying conviction of the United Nations today.

In general, later Roman Stoic literature concerned itself with daily life burdens and how to cope with them in an ethical Stoic manner. Stoicism became truly a spiritual, philosophical, and psychological pathway along which one could find tranquility and peace of mind amid the often-apparent turmoil that one became embroiled in when coping with the myriad chaotic events of imperial life.

Epictetus (c. AD 60-c. 138)

Epictetus was born during the reign of Emperor Nero, but he lived most of his life during the reign of Emperor Hadrian. He came from a Greek-speaking part of the Roman Empire, and his mother tongue was Greek. One does not know his real family name. He was a slave, and the name Epictetus means "acquired" or "obtained." While a slave, he was permitted to listen to lectures given by prominent Stoics, including Musonius Rufus. He became fascinated with Stoicism and devoted his life to its teachings.

There is a legend about him concerning an event that happened while he was still a slave. His master was twisting his leg harshly. Epictetus only smiled and calmly said, "You are going to break it." When the leg actually broke, Epictetus said quietly, "I told you so."

Around AD 89, Epictetus became a free man. He devoted his life to teaching philosophy in Rome. Philosophers were expelled from Rome during the Imperial changeover. Epictetus went to the city of Nicopolis in northern Greece. He lived the remaining years of his life there. Some say he lived in poverty. He said his possessions were only the earth, the sky, and a cloak.

Epictetus was a renowned teacher; however, he wrote nothing. His student, Flavius Arrian, took accurate and scrupulous notes of what Epictetus said. He later compiled them into books. The books were called *Discourses*. Some of them have been lost, but others have survived. The main tenets of Epictetus were put into a compendium called the *Enchiridion (Manual)*.

The following are selections from the *Discourses*:

We Are Partly Divine

If a man should be able to assent to this doctrine as he ought, that we are all sprung from God in an special way, and that God is the father both of men and of gods, I suppose that he would never have any vile or base thoughts about himself. But if Caesar should adopt you, no one could endure your arrogance; and if you know that you are the son of Zeus, will you not be elated? Yet we do not act (as if we were happy); but since these two things are mingled in the nature of man, body in common with the animals, and reason and intelligence in common with the gods, many incline to this (animal) kinship, which is miserable and mortal; and some few to that which is divine and happy.

Every man uses everything according to the opinion which he has about it, those, the few, who think they are formed for fidelity and modesty and a sure use of appearances have no base or ignoble thoughts about themselves; but with the many it is quite the contrary. For they say, "What am I? A poor, miserable man, with my wretched bit of flesh." You possess something better than your "bit of flesh." Why then do you neglect that which is better?

Stoic Apathy—We Must Exercise Ourselves against Appearances

We ought to exercise ourselves daily against appearances; for these appearances also propose questions to us. "A certain person's son is dead. Answer: the thing is not within the power of the will: it is not an evil. "A father has disinherited a certain son. What do you think of it?" It is a thing beyond the power of the will, not an evil. "Caesar has condemned a person." It is a thing beyond the power of the will, not an evil . . ." He has borne the condemnation bravely." That is a thing within the power of the will: it is a good . . . Your son is dead. What has happened? Your son is dead. Nothing more? Nothing.

How to Bear Sickness

What is it to bear a fever well? Not to blame God or man; not to be afflicted at that which happens, to expect death well and nobly, to do what must be done: when the physician comes in, not be frightened at what he says. Even if he says, "You are doing well," do not be overjoyed. For what good has he told you? When you were in health, what good was that to you? And even if he says, "You are in a bad way," do not be so sad. For what is it to be ill? Is it that you are near the rupture of the soul and the body? What harm is there in this? If you are not near that now, will you not afterward be near? Is the world going to be turned upside down when you are dead? . . . For it is not the business of a philosopher to look after these externals, neither his wine nor his oil nor his poor body, but his own ruling power.

Marcus Aurelius (AD 121-180)

Marcus Annius Verus, later to become Emperor Marcus Aurelius, was born in AD 121. He was of Spanish descent, although his family had resided in Rome for many years. His father died when Marcus Aurelius was an infant. His mother and grandfather raised him. He received a good education. He learned Latin and Greek literature, rhetoric, philosophy, and law, and he loved painting.

Marcus Aurelius was attracted to Stoicism at an early age. He studied under various famous Stoic philosophers. He was attracted to the discourses of Epictetus. Emperor Hadrian took a liking to Marcus Aurelius. He put pressure on the future emperor (Antoninus Pius) to adopt Marcus Aurelius. Marcus Aurelius in time became the sole emperor of the Roman Empire.

His reign was filled with many calamities. There were floods and famine in Italy, earthquakes in Asia, eruptions of barbarians across the borders in the north, and mutinies in Britain. He spent the last ten years of his life almost continuously away from Rome. A large part of the *Meditations of Marcus Aurelius* was written while he and his legions were battling against the Germans. He died while fighting along the Danube River in AD 180.

The Meditations of Marcus Aurelius

Gratitude

To the gods I am indebted for having good grandparents, good parents, a good sister, good teachers, good associates, good relatives and friends, nearly for every good. (*Book One*)

Right Reason

If you are doing something which is before you, *follow right reason* seriously, calmly, without allowing anything else to distract you, but keep your divine part pure, as if you were always prepared to give it back immediately. If you hold on to this, *expecting nothing*, fearing nothing, but satisfied with your present activity according to nature and with fearless truth in every word and sound which you utter, you will live happily. (*Book Three*)

Achieving Peace of Mind

Men look for retreat places for themselves, houses in the country-side, seashores, and mountains; you also want those things very much. Nevertheless this is a characteristic of the common man. It is in your power to retire into your self whenever you want. For nowhere either with more tranquility or more freedom from trouble, does a man retire into his own soul . . . I affirm *that tranquility is nothing else than the good ordering of the mind.* Give yourself this retreat constantly.

Remember to retire into this little territory of your own. Above all do not distract or strain yourself, but be free, and look at things as a man, as a human being, as a citizen, as a mortal.

Keep in mind that things do not touch the soul, for they are external and remain immovable; but our *anxieties* about them come *only* from our **judgement** which is *within*. (*Book Four*)

Inner Attitude

Time is like a river made up of the events which happen, and a violent stream; for as soon as a thing has been seen, it is carried away, and another comes in its place, and this will be carried away also. (*Book Four*)

Take away your opinion and then there is taken away the complaint, "I have been harmed." Take away the complaint, "I have been harmed," and the harm is taken away. (*Book Four*)

We Are All Fellow Citizens

If our *intellectual part is common,* the reason why we are rational beings is common. If this is true, reason which tells us what to do it also common. If this is true, there is a *common law* also; if this is so, we are *fellow-citizens;* if this is so, we are members of some political community; if this is so, the *whole world is like a state.* (*Book Four*)

Men exist for the sake of one another. Teach them then or bear with them. (*Book Eight*)

Lucius Annaeus Seneca (c. 4 BC-AD 65)

Seneca was born in Spain around 4 BC. He was a gifted writer during the Silver Age of Latin literature. He was distinguished and brilliant as a playwright, orator, and philosopher. He was perhaps "the" propagator of Roman Stoicism. When Emperor Nero was a young boy, Seneca was his private teacher. When Nero became emperor, Seneca stayed at his side as an advisor. For several years, this worked out well. Seneca seemed to be a calming influence on Nero. Seneca retired in AD 62. By AD 65, Seneca had lost the favor of Nero. He was accused of plotting against Emperor Nero. He was condemned by Nero to commit suicide for his alleged crimes. This he did in AD 65.

Seneca wrote several plays, eight of which have survived. He also wrote many letters treating of moral and ethical matters to friends in which he applies the teachings of Roman Stoicism to the crises that occur in daily life. He offers Stoic consolation in the face of grief, misfortune, and death. Providence and its influence upon all events played a central role in his thoughts.

That he was an upper class Roman and accustomed to the finer things in life created a viewpoint that there was a seeming contradiction between the teachings of Stoicism, at least in their early Greek manifestations, and the refined, cultivated, and noble lifestyle of Seneca. On the other hand, Roman Stoicism, as a moral philosophy, was a philosophy for all men to follow—rich, poor, slave, and free. The attitude that one took toward the external goods that Providence provided was uppermost and not the goods themselves. A wealthy person could view wealth as insignificant in itself and one of the less trivial externals of life. Wealth and prestige, for all of its apparent power, was still transient. With the proper attitude, everyone could become a wise person.

Seneca says,

> Do not consider him happy who is attached to external things. If you trust that joy comes from external things, you are relying upon something that is quite brittle. The joy that comes from without will disappear into the external sphere. However, what comes from within and of itself is true and constant, it increases and stays with us to the end. (*Letter to Lucilius*)

There is a legend that Seneca corresponded with St. Paul, the early Christian missionary. The correspondence between Paul and Seneca existed in the fourth century. Both Saint Jerome and Saint Augustine read the correspondence and made reference to it. Although the correspondence is considered to be apocryphal and thus not genuine, it may be an item of historical curiosity to substantiate the view that even among the ancients there existed a strain of thought that claimed Saint

Paul drew upon Roman Stoicism to illustrate the Christian moral and ethical creed.

On Giving

One is mistaken if one thinks that giving is a simple matter. There are many difficulties if one gives with deliberation and does not just squander according to chance or one's whim . . . sometimes I give out of mercy and pity, at other times I give because the person deserves the gift, so that poverty does not choke and burden him.

My gift is given in such measure that it will never be asked back, although it may be given back. An act of charity is like burying a treasure deep into the ground so that it will never be dug up again.

Generosity is not restricted to Roman citizens alone. Nature demands that it be shown to all men; whether they are slaves or freemen. (*On a Happy Life*)

On Friendship

(Lucilius) You gave your letters to a friend of yours to give to me. At the same time you warned me not to tell him everything about you that you have told me, because you have never done that yourself. You have in one and the same letter both asserted and denied that this person is your friend. You have used this word "friend" in the sense that we speak of an "unstable" friend and one whom we greet as "Sir." You are sorely mistaken if you accept someone as your friend and do not have the same trust in him as you have in yourself. You do not know the meaning of friendship.

Think seriously before you accept someone as your friend. Once you have taken someone as your friend, speak to him as openly as you would to yourself. Live as if you trust nothing and no one except your friend.

Share with your friend all your anguish, problems, and thoughts. If you treat him as trustworthy, he will become so! (*To Lucilius*)

How to Teach Philosophy

A talk that creeps into the soul in short segments is the most useful kind of talk. Long thought out and wordy lectures prepared for audiences create more noise than trust. Philosophy is good advice. No one screams out advice. Sometimes one has to use lengthy rhetoric for those who are not yet convinced of the value of philosophy. But to one who wishes to learn philosophy a serene manner of language is to be used.

The words used are like seeds that are strewn about. They are small, but if they fall into the right soil, their innate power unfolds and from a small beginning, an enormous growth develops. It is the same with the tenets of philosophy. When one looks at them, they seem insignificant. However they grow and grow in their effect. Only very little is said. However when the soul really listens to these words, it is strengthened and grows stronger and stronger. (*To Lucilius*)

Influence of Stoicism

The official "school" of Stoicism lasted for more than five hundred years in early philosophy. The works of the famous Roman Stoics were read and venerated by many Christian thinkers for centuries. Christianity differed from Stoicism in its metaphysical and theological foundation. Nonetheless, it used and still uses much of the teachings of Stoicism to explain and practice its religious beliefs. The Stoic notion of Reason (the Logos) pervading all things could easily be employed to explain the Christian belief in the Logos (i.e., Jesus Christ) as being Divine, maker of, and sustainer of the entire universe. Stoic Providence became God's Providence or God's Will guiding all things. Christianity concurred with Stoic philosophy in this respect. However, Providence was completely personalized and was understood as the Divine Providence. The Christian was to accept the events surrounding life—joy or suffering—as part of God's plan (Providence) and to submit to God's Will. God's Will is one of the great mysteries of Christian belief. Christian belief counsels that one should do his or her best and leave the rest up to Providence. Christian belief, similar to Stoic philosophical convictions, takes for granted that the world and the processes within the world are guided by a natural and eternal law.

Stoic currents of thought spread from the confines of the ancient Roman Empire to affect European philosophy in general. Traces of this influence can be discovered in the writings of later philosophers, such as Descartes, Locke, Kant, Goethe, and many others. Stoicism had its greatest effect in its relationship to Christian moral teachings. Stoicism preached an ascetic morality and disinterestedness in external goods as such. Christianity taught that one should not take external goods so seriously in comparison with the kingdom of heaven.

Christianity saw the world as striving toward a definite goal in the hands of the "Father-God." However, Roman Stoicism and the philosophical/religious beliefs were not "the same." Marcus Aurelius seems to have been rigorously against Christianity. The Roman Stoics did not wish to see their ancient religious convictions and rites destroyed by the inroads of Christian beliefs and rituals. Nevertheless, the spiritual affinities between Stoicism and Christianity remained undisturbed.

Plotinus (c. AD 204-270)

Neoplatonism may be considered the last great system of ancient philosophy. Neoplatonism, although ostensibly resting its convictions principally on the teachings of Plato, was also influenced by Stoicism and teachings from Aristotle.

One of the outstanding representatives of Neoplatonism was Plotinus. His sublime was called the *Enneads*. This was an edition of his writings put together and published by his student, Porphyry. It was a collection of the writings of Plotinus published by Porphyry thirty years after the death of Plotinus. The collection contained six sets of nine treatises, hence the name *Enneads*.

Plotinus was most probably born and raised in Egypt. When he was twenty-eight years old, he went to Alexandria. He met a philosopher, Ammonius Saccas, of whom Plotinus said, "This is the man I was looking for." Ammonius Saccas was a famous follower of the teachings of Plato. Christian philosophers also studied under Ammonius Saccas. Among them was a future Christian philosopher and scholar named Origen.

Plotinus accompanied a military expedition to Persia. The mission was ill fated, and Plotinus ended up in Rome where he founded his own circle of philosophers. Plotinus was a gentle, kindly, and honest man for whom philosophy was an experience of the meaning of life. He developed an illness near the end of his life. He moved to an out-of-the-way location and lived alone with his physician. His friends no longer visited him. His last words seem to have been, **"Try to bring back the god in you to the divine in the All."**

Plotinus attempted to live and teach the *mystical element* in Plato's philosophy. Mysticism is a phenomenon in philosophy that appears in intervals throughout the history of philosophy. It often appears in an age that has been too saturated with reason. It appears when reason seems to have failed mankind. It depicts a tendency to look for a satisfying peace of mind that slakes the inner thirst of the soul for utter fulfillment. For the mystic, reason alone is too dry and "out there." Too much reason for the mystic leads to too much uncertainty, skepticism, and desiccation of the human spirit. The mystic yearns for—and is caught up in—an *intuitive experience* of truth rather than a discursive methodical explanation of what the nature of reality is.

The mystical religions were abundant in the Roman world of the second and third century. The mystical religions emphasized certain rituals, prayers, and secret initiations through which the chosen ones might have a share in a new spiritual life. Plotinus and other Neoplatonists were neutral toward the religious rites, prayers, and initiations surrounding the mystical religions. They viewed their philosophical teachings and the practice of them as an initiation into a new and higher form of human life. The inner drives to reach a form of life beyond the sensible, to achieve a transcendent level of being, could be fulfilled by living the life and thinking the thoughts of what was considered the true philosophy.

As a mystical philosopher, Plotinus was convinced that man was divine and always remained so. He was convinced that the purpose of philosophy was to help man attain his true goal—a total and absolute union with the Good, the divine All. The purpose of his teachings was *to awaken man to a vision of his true self and the place of the human being in reality.*

Plotinus taught that fundamentally the human being's existence was a coming from and going back to the "One." His conception of the One, or of the Good, was Platonic. This One is absolute fullness and unity. He, like Plato, compared the One to the sun and sunlight. The light from the sun diffused itself and revealed the myriad things it shines upon. Plotinus states that this is the manner by which multiplicity of beings comes about. They *emanate* from *the One*. In the Platonic sense, the many things are radiated from and are reflections of *the One*. Plato taught that the "Good" penetrated into all of the ideas in the world of forms (ideas) because all of reality was "good." All ideas were "good." Plotinus experienced the "Good" (the beautiful) and the "One" as one and the same.

The One was unknowable and incomprehensible. It was beyond all being and all reality. No finite being could put into words what the "One" is, yet it exists in all things. It is sometimes called God or Father by Plotinus. Evil, for Plotinus, was a kind of Platonic "forgetfulness." Ignorance was the result of this forgetfulness. In this respect Plotinus carried on Plato's line of thinking. However, Plotinus reinterpreted this forgetfulness. Forgetfulness means to be unaware of the source of one's being. Forgetfulness means a failure to recognize (or re-recognize) the divinity within human nature. Forgetfulness is an act of the self-will that leads to ignorance.

> What can it be that has brought the souls to forget the father, God, and, though members of the Divine and entirely of that world, to ignore at once themselves and it?
>
> The evil that has overtaken them has its source in self-will, in the entry into the sphere of process, and in the primal differentiation with the desire for self ownership. They conceived a pleasure in this freedom and largely indulged their own motion; thus they were hurried down the wrong path, and

> in the end, drifting further and further, they came to lose even
> the thought of their origin in the Divine.

Although the One is the source of all being, a direct entrance into the sphere of the one is impossible. It is beyond being and beyond the knowable.

It is the initial and first "hypostasis," a Being (the term is equivocally used, as the One is beyond Being as a human being can know Being) that exists in itself. It is a substance. It exists in itself and underlies all else.

This hypostasis emanates the second hypostasis or second eternal substance. This second hypostasis is Mind or Intellect. It is the hypostasis that makes up the Platonic world of forms or ideas of which I have spoken about before. It is the sphere of the "Intelligible." Intelligible means the existence of things that *can be known*. This intelligible world stems from the One, has its eternal source in the One, and *is oriented always toward the One*. It is, however, entirely different from the One. The emanated eternal Mind is *eternally intellectualizing*. That is, it *idealizes* differences of all sorts. It idealizes movement within the infinite dimension of timelessness and eternity. This hypostasis is the Divine Mind, the Supreme Intelligence. All things are noble to this Supreme Intelligence since all things have the source of their being and intelligibility in it. Even matter and material realities are thus informed within this divine intellect.

> The greatest, later than the divine unity (One) must be the
> second of all existence, for it is that which sees the One on
> which alone it leans while the First has no need whatever of
> it. The offspring of the prior to Divine Mind can be no other
> than that Mind itself and thus is the loftiest being in the
> universe, all else following upon it—the soul, for example,
> being an utterance and act of the Intellectual Principle as that is
> an utterance and act of the One. (*Ennead V*)

The Mind emanates a third hypostasis. This third hypostasis is *Soul*. Soul is also eternal. It is the image of the Mind and eternally dependent on Mind.

But in soul the utterance is obscured, for soul is an image and must look to its own original: that Principle, on the contrary, looks to the First without mediation—thus becoming what it is—and has that vision not as from a distance but as the immediate next with nothing intervening, close to the One as Soul to it.

Soul, for all the worth we have shown to belong to it, is yet a secondary, image of the Mind: reason uttered is an image of the reason stored within the soul, and in the same way Soul is an utterance of the Mind: it is even the total of its activity, the entire stream of life sent forth by that Principle to the production of further being: it is the emanating heat of a fire which has also heat essentially inherent in itself.

Thus its substantial existence comes from the Mind; and the Reason within it becomes Act in virtue of its contemplation of that prior thing. (*Ennead V*)

From *Soul* emanates or radiates other *souls* and other realities particular realities. Soul is a world or cosmic Soul. It penetrates the entire cosmos and emanates and radiates harmony. The world *soul* contains individual souls within itself. Individual souls conjoin with matter and form the corporeal and material world.

Matter is, according to Plotinus, akin to darkness and nonbeing. It is that which is furthest from the One. Matter easily darkens the individual soul and hinders it from viewing Mind and closes off the path to intuiting the One from which it originally flowed.

The individual soul's return to the One is a process of cleansing. The inner drive is love for original beauty, harmony, and Oneness. The soul strives to overcome the shadow world of the body and return to the Spirit. The pathway is a living philosophy, meditation, and contemplation. Eventually a state of ecstasy is reached, whereby there is a total immersion into the One by an immediate apprehension of the One.

CONCLUSION

The ancient ideas concerning the meaning of, the systematization of, and the value of philosophy have never died out. More especially, the main themes of the eminent Greek philosophers have reached their zenith and nadir historically. Nevertheless, they always return to meet the needs of differing social conditions. Now pre-Socratic and Socratic thought, now the views of Plato, now Aristotle's views, now Roman Stoic views on loyalty and duty inspire insights and visions of many modern thinkers.

These ancient Western philosophies were by no means the last word on philosophy. We realize today that there will be no master plan to reveal "the truth" that will be acceptable to the whole world. We later thinkers draw upon the vivid, clear, and original insights of these ancient philosophers in a constructive way. To be blind to the positive features implanted into the universal and historically extant philosophical soil by these ancient philosophies could be seen as a mistake. These ancient philosophies have never lost their appeal for Western civilization.

SOURCES

Aquinas, Thomas. *Summa Theologiae.*

Armstrong, A. H. *The Cambridge History of Later Greek and Early Medieval Philosophy.*

The Bible.

Brumbaugh, Robert S. *The Philosophers of Greece.*

Jones, W. T. *A History of Western Philosophy.*

Jowett, Benjamin. *Dialogues of Plato.*

McKeon, Richard. *The Basic Works of Aristotle.*

Stoerig, Hans Joachim. *Kleine Weltgeschichte der Philosophie.*

Stumpf, Samuel Enoch. *Elements of Philosophy.*

About the Author

Dr. James Mittelstadt received his BA in philosophy from Immaculate Conception College. He later received his STD from the University of St. Thomas in Rome, Italy.

He has taught theology philosophy, ethics, and classical literature at numerous universities and colleges in the United States of America and in other countries.

He is now retired and lives in Samrong, Thailand.